ID0849277

King of Rock

THOMAS DUNNE BOOKS
ST. MARTIN'S PRESS
NEW YORK

King of Rock

Respect, Responsibility, and My Life with Run-DMC

Darryl McDaniels

with Bruce Haring

Foreword by Will Smith

THOMAS DUNNE BOOKS.
An imprint of St. Martin's Press.

www.stmartins.com

Design by Heidi Eriksen

Library of Congress Cataloging-in-Publication Data

DMC (Musician)
    King of rock : respect, responsibility, and my life with Run-DMC /
Darryl McDaniels with Bruce Haring.—1st ed.
        p. cm.
    ISBN 0-312-26258-2
    1. DMC (Musician) 2. Run-D.M.C. (Musical group) 3. Rap mu-
sicians—United States—Biography. I. Haring, Bruce. II. Title.

ML420.D568 A3 2001
782.421649'092—dc21
[B]   00-045964

First Edition: April 2001

10 9 8 7 6 5 4 3 2 1

This book is dedicated to
everyone who's trying to
make this world a better place to live!

Contents

Acknowledgments

There are so many people who have helped me through the years. It's impossible to list everyone right now. But I would like to take this time to thank a few special people who have been with me throughout my career and those people who have helped me with this book.

I want to first thank my wife, Zuri, for all her love and support and for always telling me to go get 'em but don't kill anyone. I want to thank my son, Dson, who loves the Beastie Boys and Backstreet Boys BUT SAYS DAD IS STILL HIS FAVORITE. I want to thank my mom and dad for teaching me respect and responsibility and my brother, Alford, who knows how to keep it real. I want to thank Tracey Miller for her inspiration and for showing me the way and Erik Blamoville for not only being a great business associate but a true friend. I want to thank Darnell Smith, who I can always count on, and give a special thanks to Will Smith for taking time out of his busy schedule to write the foreword to this book. I want to thank Loren Chodosh for not letting anyone mess with me and Janice Gartrelle Miceli for always coming through. I want to thank Bruce Haring for being my voice (it was great working with you) and Bill Adler for coaching me into a winning season. I want to thank Peter Sawyer and the Oscard Agency for their work in putting this together. I especially want to thank all the wonderful people at Thomas Dunne Books and St. Martin's Press for all their help and for being bold enough to publish these deep

Acknowledgments

thoughts. I want to take the time to thank some people on the music side, including David Reeves, who, when people had doubts, said pick that mike up and rock it; and Itaal Shur and Suzanne Hilleary for showing me the music business can be fun. Thanks to Ondi Timoner and crew for taking me to the mountain and to the ocean and showing me peace and tranquility. Thanks to Dick Allen and Ed Ryan for helping take care of my business. And a special thanks to my band—Joe, Billy, and Steve—for making some damn good music!

Foreword

I was seventeen years old when I first met Darryl McDaniels. It all started after we had gotten out of a big nasty legal situation with our record company and signed with Rush Management, operated by Russell Simmons, who also handled Run-DMC. Russell promised us we would go on tour with them. At that time, we were in one of those situations where you're feeling like it's just not going to work. Things weren't going well.

So when Russell told us that he was going to put us on tour with Run-DMC in two months, we just knew it wasn't going to happen. Everything had been going wrong, and we were absolutely positive everything was going to continue to go wrong. So going out on the road with the hottest rap group in the world didn't seem possible.

Two weeks away from the start of the tour, we're getting the tour bus, we're putting money out, and we're still convinced there's no way we're going on tour with Run-DMC. It's just not going to happen. There's no way that it's going to happen. So it started getting closer, getting closer, getting closer, to the point where now it's time to drive up to New York.

So we're like, wait a minute. How far is this joke going to go that Russell's playing on us? But we finally arrive in New York, and one of the first things we do is meet Run-DMC on their tour bus.

I'll never forget that moment they walked onto the bus. I

mean, Run-DMC . . . it was like if you're a golfer and you meet Ben Hogan, or if you're a basketball player, you meet Michael Jordan. They're all just the pinnacle of the profession. And on that bus was where I first met Darryl McDaniels.

I guess my first impression was how quiet he was. You see them on stage, and it's all screaming and energy. I just was really shocked at how laid-back and soft-spoken he was in real life. That initial impression remains true to me after all these years. Because what I discovered with Darryl is that what you see is what you get. He was always really, really friendly, really easy. He always wanted to do simpler things when we were on tour, and was really comfortable just going out to the mall rather than going to big parties. Everything was always really clear with him. You know what he's thinking and what he's feeling. If he's upset with you, he lets you know he's upset with you. When he's happy, you definitely know he's happy. If I had to sum him up, I'd say Darryl is just that dude you want in your corner. D has always got your back. He's just your man that's going to be there no matter what goes down.

He proved it to me early in our career. He always has a good word, and always wanted to make sure that we were comfortable. He took it personally that this was their tour and they wanted to make sure all the groups were cool. That's pretty unusual on the road, where the distractions and the constantly churning nature of meeting hundreds of people wears you down. That's why I'm not surprised Darryl decided to write a book about respect and responsibility. He really is concerned. He was and is concerned with everyone around him and how his actions, the steps he took and the decisions he made in his life, would affect the people around him directly and indirectly.

In short, he was responsible, and because of that, he generated respect. And that's why it's important that he write this book.

Anytime someone has followed your career and admires your work, they're always very willing to take advice on certain life situations. There's a certain level of human consideration that people give to artists in that position. Often, we fail to live up to that expectation. But the true strength of character shows up when someone can admit that, and use themselves as an example so that other people can avoid the same traps.

I really admire the strength. I don't think I could do that, at least not at this time. It's a really sensitive thing to let people know the different times when you were down, and how there's another side to the story. That's kind of a scary, vulnerable place.

But now that D has gained a greater understanding of life and his position in the world, it's time for him to share his new journey. He's searching for how he can continue to be of assistance in people's lives and make them laugh and make them smile and help them in their journeys. Just like he did to an awe-struck seventeen-year-old who got on the tour bus all those many years ago. . . .

Will Smith
July 2000

King of Rock

Introduction

You probably think you know me.

I've been a celebrity for fifteen years. Made movies, played the biggest arenas, had hit records, had videos that were in constant rotation. I've been considered a leader of hip-hop, a style and a sound that's become a worldwide, mass media phenomenon.

I'm . . . you know. The guy with the big glasses, the gold chains, and the hat.

Er . . . him.

Hey, it's okay. I get that all the time. It's funny how it works. I can walk down the streets in certain cities and have to stop every few feet to shake hands and talk with my fans. ABC TV named me one of the most important people of the twentieth century.

But some people don't know me. Others couldn't care less. Worse, they think I'm someone I'm not.

When I started out, it seemed that when anyone tried to think of my name, they would just come up with "rap." No name. Just "rap." That's what my partners, Run and Jay, would always say. Every time someone put out a "rap's greatest hits" volume or some other form of rap compilation, it always had a look-alike of me on the cover portraying a graffiti artist.

When rap got to the point where everyone had heard of it,

things got a little better. Instead of me being just a vaguely familiar face, people at least knew what I symbolized. I became the living embodiment of all things rap. "You're that rap group," people would say when they saw me in airports, restaurants, wherever. "You're the rappers. Them rappers."

That's who I was to a lot of America. "Them rappers."

Finally I decided it was time for that to change. In 1992, I revamped my image. No more hats, gold chains, and big glasses. Run, Jay, and I sought a new beginning, a new identity, a new chance. It worked. After that, people thought I was Charles Barkley because I was tall with a bald head. I'm six two and 200 pounds. Charles is six six and 270 plus.

Must have been the shoes.

So allow me to introduce myself. People call me Run-DMC. People call me Run. People call me Jay. The people who actually know who I am call me Darryl Mac, or they call me D. Very few people call me DMC, which is a nickname I created for myself in a high-school typing class, a kind of shorthand for myself.

Since we're gonna be friends for the next couple hundred pages, you can call me Darryl Mac or D. Your choice.

Although Run-DMC has been around for a long time in the entertainment business, I realize there are some people out there who haven't kept up with everything we've done over the years. Let me give you the quick highlights.

Our albums include *Run-D.M.C.* (1984), *King of Rock* (1985), *Raising Hell* (1986), *Tougher than Leather* (1988), *Back from Hell* (1990), and *Down with the King* (1993). Those albums and the singles from them have sold over twenty-five million copies worldwide. We've had a lot of firsts. Our "Rock Box" was the first rap video ever aired on MTV. We had the first rap gold album, first rap platinum album. New York *Newsday* writer Frank Owen said we were "the first rap group that really mattered."

Our *Raising Hell* album hit number three on the Billboard

top pop albums chart and was on the chart a total of seventy-one weeks. It sold over three million copies and featured the hit cover of Aerosmith's "Walk This Way." *Details* magazine named Run-DMC one of the four biggest fashion influences of the 1980s. We were the first rappers to appear on the TV shows *American Bandstand* and *Saturday Night Live*, and the first rap group to grace the covers of *Rolling Stone* and *Spin*.

In short, we've been around and done a few things. Now let me tell you a little bit about myself. I don't think I'm a complicated person. What you've seen of me on videos and in the movies and heard on records is the real me. Since the early days of my career, I've made it a point to come across in real life as what I am, an easygoing, quiet guy. I'm the rapper next door. That's why I think everybody always liked me. A lot of rappers make up an image or attitude. Me? I was always just Darryl. That's what my vocal coach says. "D, you're a friendly guy. You're always smiling and you always want to give yourself to people. People are always talking to you and you'll talk to a person as long as they hold you there."

That's why I have a vocal coach. You try talking to people for five hours as you travel about in public, then perform for three. See how your voice sounds the next day.

Now that we're acquainted, let me tell you why I decided to write this book. I've gone through a major transformation in my life over the last decade. Many things have happened within my personal life, and I believe that all things, good and bad, happen for a reason.

In my case, I refuse to acknowledge that any "bad" things have happened. So instead I'll keep it positive and say that the many things that have happened to me have all been good because they were able to bring me to this level of consciousness and awareness. I've wanted to write this book for the last eight years. The main purpose for doing so is to share the things I've learned in my twenty years with Run-DMC and my thirty plus years of living. Most of all, I want to share my awareness about two things that I believe are important in life: respect and responsibility.

If we could all have more respect for ourselves, other people, and our surroundings while taking more responsibility for our actions, then maybe as human beings we could become better citizens, better people, better friends, better lovers, and this world would be a better place for all of us. I realize that those sentiments are not new. Other people have cried out for a better mankind throughout history. But I think there's always room for more thoughts, dreams, and hopes on the subject. Because of my celebrity status, I'm often called on to comment on things that happen in the world. That's what I did on the nights when Tupac Shakur and then Biggie Smalls were killed. What struck me was that, over and over, the media asked me the same question: "Why?"

That's when I realized that I had to stand up and say something.

I started thinking we're in an endless cycle that will continue to repeat itself unless we try to do something. I realized that I don't have the magic solution or the final answer. But that night I realized that by talking about some of the things I believed needed to be said, things that some people are afraid to say because they're too worried about this week's record sales or this week's popularity poll, maybe we could all become more aware of the importance of responsibility and respect. By doing this book, I want to try to make people aware of the conditions and comments that led to the deaths of Biggie and Tupac. And more important, I want to be part of the solution, so we won't have another Tupac or Biggie situation, another attack on women, another overdose, another senseless death. And I'm not just talking about celebrities, I'm talking about the Tupacs, the Biggies, and the Eazy-E's in everyday life.

I'm tired of waiting for things to happen, then making a record about it and that's it. I say let's not wait until Thanksgiving to give out turkeys. Let's give them out every day. Things will continue to go wrong if we don't get real with reality. And that means having enough respect for ourselves to take responsibility for our actions every day, not just when tragedy strikes.

Peace,
DMC

Keeping It Real

It's funny that I've become so closely associated with rap's images. Because I never really planned on a career as a rapper.

When I was growing up, I wanted to make horror movies and bang-bang shoot-'em-up–style films. Car wrecks and the cop-and-robber movies, James Bond–type stuff. Actually, I wanted to make *and* act in movies, just what Quentin Tarantino's doing at this stage of his career. I wanted to be the creator, from start to finish. I didn't own a camera, but I had a vivid imagination. Every day of my life was a movie and I was acting out a part. My life, starring me. I would sit at home in my mom's living room, stare out the window, and draw for hours. My hometown is New York City, but there are several subsections to that description. I tell people I'm from Hollis, which is part of the larger borough of New York City known as Queens. It's a middle-class neighborhood, lots of working people. Growing up in Hollis, the biggest thing to do was hang out in the park. It was the center of public social life, a place where you would go when you had no specific plans but wanted to hook up with a bunch of your friends. It was part of my life at one point. The first thing I would do every day when I was a teenager and didn't have school was go up to the park. I'd arrive around ten-thirty, eleven in the morning and then play basketball all day. There was always someone around, looking for a game. They'd range in age from about twelve to twenty-two. At the upper end, they'd usually start going to bars, or someone had a car and they'd start hanging around outside the neighborhood.

There were actually two places that qualified as "the park" in my neighborhood. One was Jamaica Park, a public park located on Jamaica Avenue. The other was 192, actually the yard to Junior High School 192, right on Hollis Avenue. But they were both "the park" when you were asked where you'd been that day. Make no mistake, neither park was a place where you could totally let down your guard. It was dangerous. You could definitely get into trouble. You could get robbed. You could get shot. At times, it was a tense environment. Trouble could jump off, and a shoot-out could happen any minute. Somebody could like your sneakers, and then they're taking them. It was crazy. But that was probably also part of its appeal.

I started going up there around age twelve, heading up there to play ball. But I would be out of there by the evening. It was such a tense environment, I was worried that they would take my basketball. During the summer, it would start to get dark at around eight in the evening. Then you'd go home, take a shower, change clothes, and head back up to the park. Your hope at that point was that someone would be DJing in the park. Then you knew the party was on.

The DJ usually arrived in a van. It got to the point that when people saw the van, they would get really excited. They knew it was going to be a special evening.

The equipment was unloaded, they'd tap into a light pole and steal the electricity from the city, and then it was time for the party to begin.

Word would get around quickly that the van had come, and then the park would get packed. By nine-thirty, ten at night, the place would be jammed. You could hear the music for blocks, so anyone who wasn't told by a family member that the van was in the park would usually pick up on it really quick. Music was a big part of every celebration in the community, and the park wasn't the only place you could see a live DJ. Throughout the summer, the block associations would have parties where everybody would bring their little grills out and the police would come and block the whole block off. Like for instance, on 202nd Street, between 111th Avenue and 112th Avenue, that stretch of block would participate in a massive community party until about maybe seven or eight at night, when a young DJ would show up to do the same thing they would do at the park. He would set up the equipment and all the grown-ups would go inside and the younger people would take over, listening to the music, hanging out, socializing with the neighborhood kids. That's where I saw my first live DJ, at a block party. I saw him at a time when I wasn't even really thinking about hip-hop. It was before I heard one of the first hit rap songs, "Rapper's Delight," pretty much before I had any notion of the hip-hop culture. Seeing it was so different from my other music experience, which was basically listening to the radio, that it kind of caught me off guard. I thought a DJ was a guy on the radio who played records. This was something different, something exciting.

The live DJ showed me that making music didn't necessarily mean playing in a band. It was something where anyone with some equipment and some talent could make music and control a crowd's mood. I found that notion incredibly exciting and energizing. When I saw my first DJ, I thought it was amazing, but it didn't strike me at that moment that that's what I wanted to do. That came later, when I heard a tape someone had of "Superappin' " by Grandmaster Flash and the Furious Five. That's when I made the connection and knew I wanted to be a DJ. My goal was to become Grandmaster Get High, a name I bestowed on myself because that's what I was doing when I was younger.

My first hands-on music experience came as a DJ in my basement. I had two twelve-dollar turntables and a fifty-dollar mixer, and I pretended to be Grandmaster Flash, one of the first guys I heard about who was DJing by using two turntables to mix the records. That was like the biggest thing to me, the ability to cut, scratch, and otherwise manipulate the sounds contained on the records into a music composition that was wholly different. Back in those days, DJs would play music and speak to the crowd through the microphone, an all-in-one unit. Rap later evolved into two separate jobs, DJ and MC. I was an aspiring DJ at that point in my life, riding the wheels of steel, my mimic of what Grandmaster Flash called his turntable collection. At some point—I'm not sure when or why—I decided that merely spinning the records wasn't enough. I put my turntables aside and picked up a pen and paper. It proved to be the perfect outlet for my other creative energies. I had fun just writing rhymes for the sake of writing rhymes. It reminded me of my English classes at school, where they gave us creative time to just dream.

But my friend and partner, Joe Simmons (Run, as he's known worldwide, a childhood nickname because he always ran off at the mouth) wanted to be more than someone playing around in the basement. He wanted fame. He wanted to dominate in this new craft. And, fortunately, he wanted me to come along for the ride.

Run was already in show business, thanks to his brother, Russell Simmons, who since those early years has evolved into one of the most powerful people in the entertainment business. Russell now produces movies, makes records, starts magazines and advertising agencies, and generally lives large as he takes the beat from the streets and puts it on TV and elsewhere, to paraphrase one of our songs.

Back in the day, I was always over at the Simmons house. I had known Joe since kindergarten, but we really didn't become close friends until we were teenagers because we were never in the same class together. When my father put a basketball hoop up in my backyard, that's when Run and me started hanging out together, playing ball and going up to the park, doing what kids do.

And every time I was over there at the Simmons house, it seemed Russell was there. He was about six years older than us, so he had this mystique about him, something that older brothers always have. Russell was extremely funny. He may not think so, but to me, he was fun-*ny*. He was a good person to be around. Not as hectic as Run, who was always bouncing around. He was high energy, but really normal, not manic. What's unique about Russell is he was a Renaissance man of the streets. I mean, he was into hip-hop. He was into partying and had his own company, Rush Productions, that organized and promoted parties in various locations. He was into selling fake cocaine. He was into everything that a young B-boy growing up in Hollis would be into, but he was also in college and highly ambitious. He made me understand that it's possible to be from the streets yet not get caught up in the craziness of them. Russell thought everything B-boys (the name that became popular for the kind of guys you'd see hanging around neighborhoods) did was interesting, and he was into various styles of the emerging art form known as rap. He liked everything from party rappers like Kurtis Blow to more serious, message-oriented guys like Melle Mel. Larry Smith was Russell's first business partner in Rush Productions and the bass player on Kurtis Blow's "Christmas Rappin'," one of the first big rap hits. Larry always said Russell was able to come up into the Bronx and hang at a nightclub called the Fever, but also could go downtown and be at home in the Village. He could relate to both worlds and be comfortable dealing with the various characters that worked in each one. By the time we were in our teens, Russell was already well known for his work on the party circuit shows with Rush Productions. He had also starting managing artists like Kurtis Blow, who became one of the first well-known rappers in the music industry. Russell and Kurtis became tight, and Run soon became an apprentice DJ to Kurtis. Besides doing shows with Kurtis, he also began appearing on his own as DJ Run, the Son of Kurtis Blow, DJing at parties, often as the opening act for Kurtis. Run and I spent a lot of time hanging out in my basement during this period. We would go over tapes from his show, make up rhymes, ride the turntables, make up all sorts of things and plot and plan. That's what we did for recreation in those days. We were never the guys who had a lot of women in high school, or played sports, or were involved in some kind of shady activity. Sadly, if you weren't on the basketball team or running with the crew that was making money by selling reefer or whatever, girls didn't pay attention to you. That would have to wait for later in our lives.

You had a choice in our neighborhood about what kind of fun you could get into. Hollis was a nice area, but you went a few blocks in either direction and it was a lot different. A lot different. All sorts of drug sales, that kind of life. As a result, my parents, Byford and Bannah, were really strict with me. They wouldn't allow me to go out to the clubs and hear shows by rappers, or hang out all night. We had a mostly black neighborhood, but I was comfortable with all sorts of people. Even though there weren't a lot of white people in my immediate neighborhood, we'd go into those neighborhoods when I would tag along on errands with my mother and father, so I would see other sides of life. My mother was a nurse. She'd do home visitations, and occasionally I'd go with her. One of my favorite television shows when I was younger, maybe because it was set in Queens, was *All in the Family*. I remember several times going into someone's home in our territory and saying, "Dag, this is just like Archie Bunker's house," or "This man is just like Archie Bunker." What also helped broaden my perspective was reading the encyclopedia. I read the whole encyclopedia, even words I didn't know, when I was a little kid. I just found it fascinating, and each day I would go through it, volume by volume. I think that was the most fun I ever had. Although our neighborhood had its rough parts, that was good for me. I wasn't overwhelmed by it, but I got to see enough about it to know what that life was like. I know it up close and per-sonal—I had a lot of friends who ended up dead or in jail. But Run and me were going to school and avoided that sort of thing. Jay, though, was part of a really rough crew.

Even though Run and me weren't in that life, a lot of people thought we were after we became successful as Run-DMC, because we always seemed to have money and hung out with a crew that was rough. All our friends were convicts and murderers and drug dealers, but we were hanging with them anyway. We'd stand up on the corner and smoke reefer and drink beer in broad daylight for everybody to see. We sort of got a pass from people, because they were so happy to see someone from the neighborhood on TV, delivering a positive message to people.

During the initial stages of our career, I used to just walk up and down Hollis Avenue, and parents in the neighborhood would stop me to tell me that they were so proud of us. The idea was, he may still be here hanging out on Hollis Avenue, but I heard his records, and he's saying some really nice stuff.

So, go ahead, young man, smoke your reefer and hang with the guys. Because what you're saying is more important to me than what you're doing. There was definitely a stir in our neigh-borhood when Run-DMC first started to get attention. Community pride. Suddenly we were everyone's sons. Even the people who didn't exactly embrace us before were casting aside old problems and letting bygones be bygones.

There was this deli around the block from me where we used to always get our forty-ouncers. Dolly's Deli, named after the woman who manned the counter every hour of every day, trying to eke out a living. That didn't matter to a lot of kids. Every now and then there was an opportunity to steal one of the bottles, and it was an opportunity that never was passed on by a lot of us. I never did it, but it was the thing to do in the neighborhood. So it was inevitable that I would be around one day when one of my homeboys got caught. So, in essence, I would say *we* got caught. He ran in there and took two, then brought them around the corner, went back in and got another two. Then he did it again, a total of six. I guess on the last go-round they saw him. So Dolly came around the corner with her gun and began yelling at all of us. "Don't y'all ever come in here again, never!" Really mad and upset. So, at that moment, I was banned from Dolly's.

That happened when I was sixteen years old. Two years later, it was the last day of high school, which had seemed like it would never arrive. My friend Douglas Hayes and I were feeling cocky, what with school ending and all. So we decided to try our luck and see if Dolly's had either forgiven or forgotten.

They hadn't. They told us we couldn't come in there. So a few months go by, and I'm in college. Our record starts blowing up on the radio, and so we decided to check it out and see if Dolly's lifetime ban was still in effect.

Well, we walk in there, and it's a whole different story now. I'm no longer Darryl, the accomplice. I'm now Mr. DMC from Hollis, Queens, the man with the record on the radio. Whole different attitude, take anything you want, do what you want. It's strange how that goes. Everybody wanted to be my friend. People that wouldn't give me the time of day before were suddenly eager to help me out. Most of the guys that I couldn't hang with back in the day, all of a sudden, I'm down. All of a sudden I am able to ride with them to Jamaica Avenue. All of a sudden I'm able to come on their side of the park. That happened pretty much immediately after the album came out. Once that album came out, the video followed, it was over. Everybody wanted to fall down and cater to us. Women suddenly wanted to be with Darryl from Hollis. All of a sudden they want to be my friend, they want to be my homeboy, they want to drink a beer with me. One of the main things that happened was that people started asking me for money. A lot of people in the neighborhood, the hoodlums, the lowlifes, a lot of the older girls. Everybody.

And you get them real pissed off when you don't come across with it. "Oh, you think you're so big! You think you somebody? Well, you ain't nobody!" I got that routine a lot. I always thought, "If I'm nobody, why the hell are you nagging me!"

Basically, it all boiled down to a simple lesson: if you've got something somebody wants, they start acting differently. I noticed that aspect of life even before it happened to me. That's why the attention never rubbed off on me. I had already given it some thought and was prepared to understand what was happening and why it was happening. I understood that it wasn't like I woke up one morning and suddenly was transformed. It wasn't even that I was a wonderful person before that no one had noticed, but that they suddenly became aware of because of the record. No, it was the fact that it was now safe to voice your opinion of me. I had been validated by the mass audience, so now it became easy to be my friend. There was no risk involved, and potential rewards—money, the chance to do something that you wouldn't normally do, maybe meet a few stars. I held the key to a new kingdom, and everyone wanted to step through that doorway with DMC, getting a little of the spoils. My family helped keep me grounded. My family was always normal, never started acting different once I made the record. In fact, my mother would warn me, "Watch out for those people, because they're only around you now because you're famous."

A lot of today's athletes and musicians don't have someone like my mother around to tell them that. I see how a lot of these young basketball players and young football players can become caught up in all the attention. I remember watching one guy on TV saying how his family just flipped on him.

I understand where he's coming from. Even though my family remained normal, the world seemed ready to roll out the red carpet. And if you're not prepared for that, it can really play with your head. Even today, I still get that treatment. I can walk into any store, they'll find out it's me, and they'll probably give me stuff free. The opposite is true as well. People will still come up to you as though you're a walking ATM.

The other day I was in Atlanta, walking through a mall there that I like to shop at when I'm in town. And as I was walking through the mall, this guy came up to me, giving me all these props, laying it on real thick. Then he pulls out his little cassette and says, "Yo, buy a cassette for five dollars."

I'm like, "No, I'll take it and listen to it and give you some advice." But buying it wasn't something I was down with. He wouldn't take no for an answer. "Aw, no, man, you rich," going on and on, this and that. It got to the point where I had to set him straight. The bottom line: don't think I'm rich. A lot of people coming up in the game now, they the ones making millions. But back in the day, when I came up in the eighties, we were struggling. Most of my money is made by doing live performances. I'm not making money off my album sales. A lot of people just don't understand that. Maybe if more of them did, they'd start to examine whether they want to be friends with DMC, or Darryl. I want people to like me because I'm Darryl. The other guy only exists at the live shows.

Anyway, me and most of my friends didn't really have a grand plan after high school. We were going to college pretty much because it was what we knew how to do. We'd figure out later just what it was we were searching for.

But even though we didn't do much calculation, our music career just seemed to evolve around us. I remember the first time Run and me performed together. It was at the Le Chateau on Hillside Avenue in Queens, in 1981. Run was doing a show in his guise as DJ Run, the Son of Kurtis Blow, opening for this other rapper, Sweet G., who had a record that was popular at the time. Little did I know that it was going to be the most important moment of my life.

It started out as a normal day. I was a junior in high school, seventeen years old, so that meant come home from school, do your homework, grab something to eat, and then go outside and get high.

This was a Friday, so I was relaxing a bit at home when Joe called me. "Yo, D, I got a show at the Le Chalet. You know where that's at, right?"

Yeah, I knew. I figured he wanted me to come down and check it out. I was surprised to hear what he said next. "I want you to come and be down with me. I got DJ Kippy-O. I want you to come and be down with me."

I paused for a second. I mean, we had been playing around in my basement for a while, rhyming and getting high and having fun. But now . . . I'm like, "What?" That was all I could say. Joe was adamant. "I want you to come and be at my house at such and such a time." He loved the raps we had done in my basement and his attic so much, he wanted to incorporate them into his show. I didn't know what to say, so I agreed. "All right. All right. Cool."

I hung up the phone and was filled with dread. It never occurred to me that he would call me and say, "Yo, come do this show with me."

Oh, man. I sat down for a minute. I was so scared, I felt like I was in a daze. It was one thing to goof around in my basement, making things up on the fly. Now I was going to have to do it in front of other people, maybe a lot of other people, some of whom wouldn't be so kind when what I was creating on the spot didn't work. What had I agreed to do? I really, really, really didn't want to get up and rap in front of people. I liked rapping in my basement. That was my whole thing. But now . . . am I going to be good? What's going to happen when I have to do this in front of people who expect to be entertained?

I knew what I had to do. I had to go get confident. So I

headed down to my basement to get me some Southern Comfort. We used to drink and get high when we played around in Joe's attic and my basement. We would sit around and turn on the turntables and rap and scratch all night. That's after drinking forties and smoking cheeba all day. I'd have a few hits and then say fifty rhymes off the top of the head. So I felt if I drink a lot tonight, it's going to make me even better.

That's what my mentality was at the time. I'll go down to the basement and get some Southern Comfort, drink half the bottle. I'll be Superman, ready to conquer the world. I'm down there in the basement, just me and my thoughts. My mom was already in bed. She would go to bed at six o'clock, seven o'clock on school nights, because she had to get up early and make breakfast before heading to work. My dad left for work at 4:00 P.M. I never told my parents where I was going that evening. They wouldn't have let me go down to a nightclub if they knew that's where I was going. If I ever came home late, I'd just tell them I was down at the park. Finally, after hours of drinking, it was time to head over to Joe's. I lived on 197th Street, he lived on 205th, maybe a ten- or fifteen-minute walk away. That walk proved to be the most important fifteen minutes of my life. On the way there, I was going through all the rhymes that I ever made up. Which ones would I say? Would I remember all my lines? Would people get into it? My thing was, certain rhymes were written for certain records. I had one style of rhyme if I'm rhyming over Billy Squier's "Big Beat," another if I'm over "Rocket in the Pocket" by Cerrone. What if they don't play a record I can rhyme to? These are all the things that were racing through my mind. And as I'm walking, I remember thinking, "Man, I am drunk," which kind of amplified all of my questions. Finally I reached his block. This was the moment of truth. I remember getting halfway up the block and wanting to turn around and go home. Every step was like I was on my way to my execution.

It was a dark night, which might have added to the sense that I was moving into something fearful, something unknown. Each step brought a question. Should I go home? I don't want to do this. I can't do this. At one point, I actually turned around and started walking home.

But something stopped me. It's hard to put into words, but I knew that I would be forever ashamed of myself if I didn't at least try. I had to know whether I could do this. As comforting as it would be to just walk home and not do it, I couldn't live with myself if I copped out and made up some excuse. There I was, in the middle of 205th Street, pitch black on a Friday evening, struggling with myself.

I'll go. No, let me go home. No. I won't. I went through that push/pull struggle. Finally I summoned my courage. I went up the driveway and knocked on the door. There was no turning back at that moment. The funny thing is when I got there, Joe didn't know I was drunk. He was like, "You want something to drink?" I was like, "Cool. Yeah, give me a lot." So by the time we got to the club, I was so loaded I don't even remember what happened between leaving Run's house and arriving there. Sadly, I don't remember much else at that point about what happened at the club. I do remember when it was time for us to go up, I went and sat down by the side of the stage behind the speaker. I don't remember how I knew it was time to come in, but I remember the song "Seven Minutes of Funk" being on. There's some vague recollection of Run rhyming my intro, "Easy D, my man / when you're ready / get on the mike with the master plan." It was early, so there wasn't much of a crowd in the club. Still, I couldn't manage to rouse myself enough to get up on the stage. So I sat at the side of the stage and did my rhymes next to the speaker.

I rapped for maybe a minute out of Run's fifteen-minute set. It probably wasn't brilliant compared to the clever things I was coming up with in my house, away from the crowd. But it seemed to work for the setting and the few people that were in the club that night. I was so drunk, it all blurs together. I think I had wanted to go up there and say every rhyme I had ever wanted to to say, but I couldn't get it out. I was blind drunk. I couldn't see. I don't even know how I managed to stay on the beat.

I must have done all right, though. The next day, Joe told

me, "Yo, D, you was real drunk because you sat by the side." I
didn't know that until he told me. "You don't know what you did?"
"What'd I do?" But I guess I was on because he didn't say I messed
up. He just said the worst thing I could do was sit on the side of
the stage and not look at the crowd, and he gave me some point-
ers. He was like, "Next time, sit in front of the stage" and "You
could have had your hood over your head."

I do remember leaving the club. I remember that because it was
the biggest relief of all time. It's over. I had survived. My senses
briefly revived as Joe gave me ten dollars, so I went and bought
some Bacardi rum. The feeling was that I had done it, even
though I wasn't quite sure what I had done. But I definitely had
the feeling that I did it. I had been thrown into the arena and
lived to tell the tale. After the performance, I woke up out of the
dream. I left there with a sense of accomplishment. I had survived! Now let me just move on.

Unfortunately, getting really drunk before performing became a habit that I grew to rely on. One of the first shows that
me and Run ever did as Run-DMC was at the Roxy nightclub in
New York, back in 1983, when we released our first record. The
show was attended by what seemed like the whole Zulu Nation,
one of the most powerful street gangs in the city, led by DJ Afrika
Bambaataa, who had one of the first rap hits with "Planet Rock."

I had to drink a fifth of Southern Comfort to make it to that
show, again justifying it to myself because I needed confidence. It
worked, but soon I realized every time I had to go somewhere or
make an appearance, I had to have that drink, because that was
my confidence. I needed that confidence. That wasn't the right
way to look at things. But I'll talk later about that.

I remember the day I got the call from Joe to come into the
recording studio to make "It's Like That" and "Sucker M.C.'s."

Joe made the call, but I later learned that the only reason I was at the recording session is because he insisted on it. His brother, Russell, didn't think I added anything to the mix.

Russell was focused on Run's career in the early days. Originally Russell was going to have Run front this group called the OK Crew (for Orange Krush), pairing him with people Russell had met from his party promotion crew, people he was hanging around, people he met through DJ Kurtis Blow and another popular performer, DJ Hollywood.

But Russell was too influenced by the type of music he was hearing at the parties he promoted, and that wasn't the type of music Run wanted to make. He didn't want to be like Kurtis Blow, rapping over "Good Times" and making R & B records. Run wanted to be like the Funky Four Plus One and the Cold Crush Brothers. He wanted to do the hard, rough raps that we used to do in the park when we were hanging out.

Russell didn't want Run doing what we were doing in the basement and the attic. Russell was into DJ Hollywood and Kurtis Blow. He was promoting parties with Kurtis Blow, DJ Hollywood, and Eddie Cheeba, top-shelf shows at places like the Hotel Diplomat and the Fantasia. Although those places could attract a rough crowd at times, Russell was competing with the real hard places in the Bronx and in Harlem. He was doing college parties, not dealing with clubs that catered to gangs. Thus, when it came time for his brother to record, Russell was pushing one style, his brother wanted to do another. I guess Joe felt he needed a friend there to back him up, someone whose taste mirrored his, so that he could get Russell to change his mind.

Even though I knew those records Russell loved like the back of my hand, I was also more intrigued with the hard-edged street rappers that I heard on these bootleg tapes I was getting from guys in my high school. Live performances of Afrika Bambaataa, Melle Mel, Cold Crush, Kool Moe Dee. Not the soft, party rappers. Run and I wanted to be something else, the guys who took what we were hearing on the streets and in the park to a new level.

Even though Russell had a different taste in music, he listened to his brother. In the end, he was all about helping his brother start a career in whatever style he wanted to do.

But when he looked at me, he wasn't as impressed with my potential. In fact, he didn't think I had a voice at all, although he did admire my sense of style in clothes and my attitude. He used to test records with me all the time, even though we had different tastes.

Russell was always saying, "D will never be a rapper. But if he nods his head to a beat or a record, it's def." He also liked the way I would always wear sweatshirts with hoods and have my pants hanging off my butt. That was all interesting to him, yet another bit of culture that he could appreciate.

But if it wasn't for Run insisting that I had to be on a record with him, I wouldn't have had a chance. And my life would have been far different.

In the Beginning

In 1983, Run was in school at LaGuardia Community College. He was studying mortuary science. I was in St. John's, working on a business management degree.

Run always insisted he was going to make a record, but he had to wait to get out of high school first. It was his father's influence. His father was supervisor of attendance for School District 29 and taught black history at Pace University. Plus, Russell told him that he needed something to fall back on in case show business didn't work out.

Like I said, at first Run was going to be down with a crew and they was going to call it the OK Crew. It was going to be Run, this girl DJ from years ago called Lady Blue, and some other rapper.

Of course, soon enough Run changed that. He was going to call the group DJ Run.

Although Run had his own thing going, he was always encouraging me. "D, you can rap and DJ and you just have so many rhymes, we can go get paid 'cause your ideas are crazy."

One day, he put that encouragement to the test. Run called me up. "D, I'm really going to make a record this weekend. It's called 'It's Like That.' "

He had some ideas for lyrics on the song, but he needed help. "Just write, D. I know you can write, 'cause that's all you do," he told me. "Go home and write about how the world is. Write a bunch of rhymes about that."

That was my assignment.

Rap came to me easily because I always viewed it as an extension of schoolwork, which I enjoyed and was good at. So I went home and wrote all these rhymes.

Run was ecstatic when he saw the results. "These are great, D! We're going to make that record!"

But something still didn't feel right about "It's Like That." I thought it over that night after showing Run the lyrics. The next day I called him again.

"I'm thinking, when you go 'It's like that,' I think there should be something to answer," I said. Then I fed him my idea: "It's like that / And that's the way it is."

When I said it, something clicked. I thought we had something special. I was right.

Russell was shown the lyrics the day after that phone conversation, and he encouraged us to record it.

Actually, he encouraged Run to record it. But my man insisted that he wanted to work with me. Run told his brother, "I'm not making a record unless you put D on it."

Case closed. We were officially a team.

When we first started, the take we had on rap music was that everybody who was big in it at the time, acts like Grandmaster Flash, Sugarhill Gang, Kurtis Blow, all of the early rappers, were fake. They're not doing what we were growing up doing in the park, we said. Although they came from that kind of atmosphere, the street parties and park throwdowns, when they went to make their records, they became something else.

It was our desire to present to the world what was being done in our basements and in our parks. I think that's one of the reasons why people think they really knew me, because always in my lyrics, I would talk about everyday things. "My mother cooking chicken and collard greens. . . ."

My rhymes were never really to the point of braggadocio. I always said stuff that people either lived or could relate to me saying. And it was like by me saying all this, it's like they lived with me and became part of my life.

The way we came up with "It's Like That" is basically the pattern that we followed throughout our songwriting career. Run would tell me, "D, write about this." I'd get to work, find some inspiration, and then we'd go and make records.

When it was time to record, they'd usually tell me, "D, bring your rhyme book to the studio." And Russell and Larry Smith, who supervised a lot of the sessions, used to go through my lyrics, picking and choosing.

"Oh, that's a record."

"Yeah, that's one!"

They used to pull the titles for the records from phrases I would write. Like our second big hit, "King of Rock." Originally I had written, "I'm the king of rap / there's none higher. . . ."

But Russell had a better take on it. "No. We're going to take that, and we're going to put it in the front of the song and change rap to rock." He was right on that call, and "King of Rock" became another huge record.

That's how the hits were made, Russell and Larry going through the book, taking my lyrics, and we'd put them over beats.

Getting the rest of our act together was also pretty simple.

The way we dressed was how we used to dress in junior high school. The whole neighborhood used to wear hats and big gold chains. But that wasn't the first thing we tried.

The origin of how Run-DMC began to get its style together starts at one of the clubs we played back in the early days. It was called the Disco Fever, a little club up in the Bronx on Westchester Avenue. It was into rap music very early, and so it became the hangout for guys like Grandmaster Flash, Melle Mel, Cold Crush, whoever was making records then.

This was *the* stop for aspiring young artists. You could go and see Grandmaster Flash DJing one night. You could go there and see Starsky DJing one night. It was ground zero for rap at that point in its development.

But the club was also a big spot for drugs. And all sorts of characters would hang there. You go in there and get high as hell, drink, and just have fun in whatever way you wanted to have fun.

Places like the Fever, you play and get your pay and when you get outside the front door, the stickup kids are right there. "Give it up."

Luckily we had Jay and knew a lot of the drug dealers that were hanging out in the Fever. That, and the fact that a couple of drug dealers from Queens would go to the Fever, made us all right.

Naturally, with all this excitement and danger around it, playing the Disco Fever was huge. So when our record first came out, before we even had the album, we were excited when we were booked to play at the Fever.

There was just one problem. This was so early in our career, we didn't quite have our image together. So, still experimenting, we decided to wear these checkered suit jackets.

I think it was Run's idea, because at the time, people in the hood were wearing these checkered cloth blazers. I mean, this was retro—as a matter of fact, I went and found mine in my father's closet.

That was my first mistake. It wasn't like the hip checkered

jackets, the ones you could buy off Jamaica Avenue where we shop. No, this was from my dad's closet.

There was something about that jacket that didn't feel right. But like I said, we were trying different things out, so somehow we convinced ourselves that this was the look, that it made us regular.

Just before the date, we got some bad news. Jay wouldn't be able to make it, so we had to use the in-house DJ.

So here we are, one of the most eagerly anticipated shows of our early career, and we're already feeling kind of strange, dressed in these outfits and without our regular DJ and security enforcer.

But it's on with the show. We soon found ourselves backstage at the club, all nervous as we're ready to go on.

Finally we're introduced to the crowd with a booming welcome.

"Here they are, Run-DMC, these guys have a new record out, from Queens, New York, Run-DMC."

I don't know what the crowd was expecting. I guess they thought we'd look like Grandmaster Flash or Afrika Bambaataa or Kurtis Blow, the gods back then in rapping.

We walk out onstage with these checkered jackets. I had a yellow, green, and brown checkered jacket, matched with a tan, mock neck sweater, green Lee jeans with blue Pumas with the white stripes. And I think Joe had on a black and grey checkered jacket, a black mock neck, light gray Lees, and white Adidas with the black stripes.

Everything just got really quiet. It was like the people in the seats looked at us and said, "What the hell is this?"

It was a strange feeling for me and Joe. You could almost hear crickets chirping when we walk out after the intro, then it got to the point where you could hear a pin drop, and then we heard a couple of homies laughing at us.

We knew instantly what the problem was. But we were too embarrassed to turn around and run offstage too. Okay, we're chumping ourselves, but running offstage would have been worse.

So then the record dropped, and we managed to bring the crowd back a bit. But overall, it was mixed. The only thing that saved us was our reputation: this is the group from Queens with that hot record. We already had one strike against us because we were from Queens, because all the rappers in the Bronx and Manhattan were mad at these new jacks, who were actually doing what they were doing, but doing it on a record.

That show was almost the end of Run-DMC. I was like, I really don't want to be up there rapping. I was like, I don't like this. I'd rather stay in my basement and rap and not have to worry about how I'm going to look in front of people.

But Joe had other ideas. He was used to this sort of thing, having already done a lot of shows with Kurtis Blow. He set me straight: don't worry about it. Wear your hat and just go get a solid-color jacket.

That marked the evolution of our stage gear. We were going to be comfortable in what we wore, adopting a lot of what we would usually wear on the street to the stage. So we went out and I think I got an all-blue blazer, and I wore it with my black Lees and my black-and-white Adidas. Joe got a black blazer and he wore black Lees.

Joe also insisted that hats were what we had to wear. "D, you always wear a hat! You got to wear a hat!" So I started wearing a Kangol Apple Jack. We got it right after that show and our next show was a show with Kool Moe Dee and the Treacherous Three.

This time, we came correct with our look and were able to handle it. Eventually we dressed more and more in regular street clothes, adding little touches here and there like the chains.

Russell really liked it, thought it was fascinating, and decreed that that's how we were going to dress onstage. Like our music, our look would be from the streets. We were keeping it real.

One important piece of that stage attire—the most important piece, as far as the public is concerned when they think of me—came from Run's inspiration.

I had taken to wearing Cazal-like glasses on occasion. Run was struck by them.

In the Beginning

"D, put your glasses on for a second. Yo! Those are the coolest thing, man. Those are big!" So that's how my glasses stuck and became my trademark. I wouldn't wear them constantly, but that became my image. It was a fad that also became popular among the B-boys, who thought the glasses were as much of a prop as the gold chains.

What made Run-DMC work is everybody put in what they could offer. I was the lyricist; Run had ideas and lyrics; and Russell, as a manager, got on the phone and screamed our way to success.

Thanks to Russell's hustling, we hooked up with Profile Records, a small independent record label that was just getting started in New York City.

Russell shopped and shopped before we got the deal, wearing out the phone books looking for a label that was interested in our music. Russell already had scored the first rap artist to sign to a major label when he got Kurtis Blow a deal with Mercury Records, one of the oldest imprints in music.

But for some reason he was having difficulty getting us signed. Kurtis Blow had a track record with the hits "The Breaks" and "Christmas Rappin' " before he signed to Mercury, so maybe the labels thought there was something there. But rap music in general? They thought it wasn't going to last.

We had never heard of Profile Records, but I liked the vibe when I finally went in to meet them. It was three guys, Cory Robbins, Manny Bella, and Steve Plotnicki. They came across as cool. They were very young looking, and everything about the record business was just as fresh to them as it was to us.

Not that I had many options, but it just wasn't all that important to me which label we signed with at that point. I didn't really think about rapping as a career. When we signed to Profile, it wasn't treated like I was signing to Motown to become the next Jackson 5.

My attitude was, we were just rapping in my basement, and now they're going to put it on a record, the same way Cold Crush puts it on a tape. That's nice.

But I soon learned how big a deal it really was. "It's Like That" / "Sucker M.C.'s," our single, was released in March 1983 and went to number fifteen on the Billboard R & B chart, an almost unheard-of height for a rap single at that time. "Sucker M.C.'s," which we originally thought was just a throwaway B side, received strong praise as well.

Both songs were featured again in March of 1984 on our debut album, appropriately titled *Run-D.M.C.* produced by Russell Simmons and Larry Smith. It became our and the label's first big hit, scoring a gold record, 500,000 units sold. It was the first rap album to go gold, and we were the first rap group to have a video on MTV.

How we got our name is another matter.

One day, me, Run, and Larry Smith were at Larry's house in Queens. We were busy making the tracks to what became "It's Like That." It was a hot day, and we were up there in Larry's attic.

Russell wasn't there, but he was on the job. He called that day with an announcement. "Yo! The name of the crew is going to be Run-DMC." I wish the whole world was in the room that day, when Russell first said that.

"See? It sounds so good. Run-DMC." I can almost hear him now. We looked at each other.

I can't even say it the way he did, but our first reaction was that it sounded nasty, ugly, stupid. Me and Run were almost in tears.

"Russell. You ruining us! It's stupid . . . it . . . Run-DMC?"

Grandmaster Flash and the Furious Five. DJ Afrika Bambaataa and the Zulu Nation. The Fearless Four. The Treacherous Three. The Sure Shot Crew. The Magnificent Seven MCs. The Two MCs. Double Trouble. Those are names.

Not Run-DMC. What does that mean? It sounds so stupid!

We could have really fought. I don't know. We just gave up on it. We just really gave up on it.

In the Beginning

We recorded our first two records without Jay, but we knew we needed a DJ. We knew Jay from the neighborhood. He was already working in two groups as a DJ, one of them called Two-Fifth Down. They were like the neighborhood DJs and MCs who'd set up their equipment in the park and pull a park jam. And you hired them to do the house parties.

At first, the guy who was Jay's technical assistant, Nellie D, was going to be our DJ because Jay was busy with two groups.

But when it came time to make the decision, Run lobbied hard for Jay. The reasons had as much to do with who he was as his talent.

Jay was living the thug life in our neighborhood way before it was popular. I mean, Nellie D was a thug, but he wasn't thugged-out like Jay, who learned at an early age that he had to project a wild image in order to avoid having people running up on him all the time.

Jay hung with a tough crowd that was actually out doing all the things that a lot of gangsta rappers later put on records. But Run figured if we put Jay in the group, nobody's going to mess with us. Nobody's going to stick us up. Nobody's going to rob us. Nobody's going to diss us. All the thugs that were his friends would come to the shows as well.

So he was brought on for reputation and enforcement. That put the whole Hollis crew behind us, and they became our free security.

I nicknamed Jay "Jam Master." It sounded good. I had picked up DMC in a typing class, a way to shorten my name. And Run, as mentioned, had his nickname since childhood.

But we still were debating what the group would become. How are we going to go about this? What's the vibe?

One thing didn't change when Jay became the DJ. It didn't become Run-DMC and Jam Master Jay—it was just Run-DMC, even though there were three of us. Which caused a lot of confusion for people.

We saw all sorts of weird combinations of our name. People

thought the group was Run-MC. They thought it was one person, Run the MC. Or people thought it was Run, a guy named D, a guy named M, and a guy named C.

When we had "It's Like That" out, we used to always do a lot of shows down in Florida and other points south of Atlanta. For some reason, that region of the country seemed to have the hardest time grasping what our name was. Everybody used to come up, "I know this is Run. But which is D? Who's M? And where's C at? Why's there only three of y'all? Ain't there a fourth guy? Run, D, M, and C?"

In the end, it became funny to us, and the name grew on us, becoming cool. Run-DMC. It was kind of rock-and-rollish. And whether there were three members, four members, or seven, it was still going to be called Run-DMC.

I was a business management student at St. John's University when the group started. Why St. John's? Me and my friend, Butter, whose real name was Doug Hayes, wanted to go to the same school.

Why business management? The guidance people asked me right around high-school graduation to pick something to write in on my college application. I was tired that day, and business management was near the top of the list. So I checked it off.

To tell you the truth, I wasn't real big on college, even though I had enjoyed school to that point. I had excellent grades and was good at rhyming and drawing, but I didn't know what I was going to do with my life. School seemed like it would fill that gap for the moment.

Thank God the music career worked out. I only worked one day job in my life.

My friend and I were supposed to hand out flyers. We threw them in the garbage. The guy who hired us saw us do this. End of job. Who's to say where I'd be today if it wasn't for that break?

In the Beginning

I'll never forget the moment when I first heard our music on the radio. I was home in Hollis, in my room, and my mother and father were next door in their bedroom, my brother was somewhere else in the house. It was about eight in the evening, and I had on WRKS, KISS-FM, 98.7.

I knew there was a chance that our record would be picked up, but I wasn't monitoring the radio station. I just happened to be listening because it was one of my favorite stations.

I don't remember how the jock intro'd it. It was something like "Here's something brand-new," something like that. That's all I remember. I must have blanked because when I heard the beats, I knew it was me.

"Ma!" I shouted. "I'm on the radio! Come listen! Yo, check it out! Yo! Alford!"

Three minutes later my partner, Run, called. He was also home listening (okay, maybe we were monitoring). "D!!!" he was shouting. "It's, it's. . . ."

I just shouted back, "I know, I know. I'll call you back afterwards."

After that, I sat there and waited to hear it again. They quickly put it into rotation, and I heard it in the afternoon, and then I heard it like 6:30 P.M., then I heard it again at 9:30 P.M.

That was the beginning. But it was also the end of something.

I went to St. John's for two semesters, but early in the second semester, "It's Like That"/"Sucker M.C.'s" came out. I was doing fairly well in college until that point, but I started to slip in my attendance because I wasn't really into it. It was really a strict school, so the dean actually called my house because I was cutting classes.

That was kind of the turning point for me. When they called, I had to make my decision and inform my parents. It was not a talk I was looking forward to having, but I felt I had to be a man about it and tell them straight up, "I want to make records."

I resolved that I was going to present it to them as a leave of absence. I'd keep the door open to returning to college, just in case things didn't work out.

I was lucky we had a show coming up. We were ready to go to North Carolina, so I didn't have to be around the house and provide a convenient target after I told them.

They weren't happy with my decision, but they agreed that I could do it. They said, "All right, take a leave of absence. But remember, you're going to go back." That was the thing they kept saying. "You're going to go back." Even talking about it later, when my career started to pick up some momentum. "You're going to go back to it."

Although our first record was successful, it didn't take off like a rocket. I was walking through college and "Sucker M.C.'s" or "It's Like That" would be playing on the college PA system. I would be sitting there in the cafeteria, but nobody knew it was me. I'm in my own little world saying, "That's me." I wasn't the type of guy to go around pounding my chest, yelling "Yo! That's my record!"

Actually, we really didn't get any public acknowledgment until the first album and the "Rock Box" video.

I was driving in my car one day on the highway. I was driving along, you know, playing my booming system, when I noticed this car on my side. I guess they probably had been trying to get my attention for the last ten miles or so.

So I'm looking over and they're looking at me and I'm driving.

It was a carload of young girls. One of them rolled down the window.

"Are you Run-DMC?"

"Yeah."

Everybody in her car screamed. You know, "Yahhhhhhhhh!"

Oh, yeah. They were paying attention now.

Finally all that attention on the basketball and street guys switched to us. I started noticing it walking down Jamaica Avenue. You know what I'm saying: it was that feeling like, "Women are lookin'. . . ."

But there were some other lessons I was about to learn as we started getting more popular.

In the Beginning

It was 1985, the first major rap tour, the Fresh Fest. I was eighteen.

It was, in a word, wow.

Our manager, Russell Simmons, got together with some of the biggest black promoters of the time and scheduled a tour in the biggest arenas with the hottest groups of the moment, a massive celebration of the hip-hop culture of the moment.

The lineup was Run-DMC, Whodini, Kurtis Blow. We had break-dancers, we had double-Dutch groups, we had ten-year-old Jermaine Dupri, who's a big record producer now, come out and open up with some dancing. We had the Fat Boys, who were really big at the time. Well, they were just really big, but, you know. . . .

In short, it was *the show*.

This was the life I grew up watching on all those rock 'n' roll documentaries. It was like the Rolling Stones and the Beatles, traveling the country, playing the big coliseums and civic centers in every major city. It was all new to me. For instance, I found out what a tour bus was. I was used to the Trailways and Greyhounds. But now we had a bus with beds and bathrooms and VCRs.

And there was one other thing that was introduced to me about the big time—the amount of drugs that were freely available.

I wasn't a drug virgin. Getting high was part of our lives, like going to school, doing our chores, respecting our community, and minding our parents. It wasn't anything we particularly thought about. It was just part of growing up in my neighborhood.

Then when we started making records, I was making money. We always talked about getting paid. It meant we could get more cocaine, reefer, beer, cigarettes, whatever. This may seem decadent to you, but it was just everyday stuff to us. Everyone was doing it. No big deal.

But all I knew about back in my neighborhood was dimes—ten-dollar bags of marijuana—and little vials of cocaine, things that are mainly used for recreational purposes at parties and hanging out.

On this tour, I found out what an eight ball of cocaine was. Whoa, did I find out.

Every town you go into, the drug dealers are right there, hanging out, selling their stuff, doing their stuff with you, buying another round of drinks.

But even in the early days of the Fresh Fest tour, when we were partying pretty hard by my standards, I started hearing about Miami.

This was the time when *Miami Vice* was on TV, so we all had an image of what was there. But I was hearing about a different kind of Miami from people older than me who were on the tour, people who had been on the road and done shows there. "When we get to Miami," they'd say, arching their eyebrows. "Oh, when we get to Miami. . . ."

So we got to Miami. And nobody went to bed.

Just about everybody on the tour stayed up the entire three days getting high. I mean, real high. Constantly sniffing, day and night.

Despite my experimentation, I had never sniffed that much coke, never drank that much, never hung out all that late. In Miami, we had two shows, and they proved to me that there was a world out there that was beyond anything I could have imagined when I was playing in my basement in Hollis.

Backstage at those shows, all the drug dealers, the high rollers, all those people I wouldn't have gotten to hang out with if I wasn't on that tour, all of them came around. Some deep people. Yes, very deep, the kind of people you'd see on *Miami Vice.*

I saw a lot of things and learned a lot in those two days.

For instance, I didn't know the security people got high. I could just go up to one of the guards and say "Yo! Here's three hundred dollars. Whatever you get tonight, make sure you get me some and come see me after the show." No problem, they'd say. It was like ordering a pizza to them.

I felt kind of like a young kid back then, and it was amazing to me to see men partying, because I would always say to my friends that you don't get high forever. But then here I am in

Miami and I'm looking at guys around forty-five years old and older getting high and drinking and hanging backstage with us. There went that theory.

I'm telling you, it was excessive. Real heavy. Everything was done at binge levels. A lot of money was being made on that tour, so there wasn't just a little bit of drugs or liquor. The whole tour was like that.

You know, I think I probably started gaining weight during that Fresh Fest tour because I wouldn't just buy one cheeseburger or one meal. I'd buy four. You know, I look back and say a lot of us could have died, the way it was.

We were standing on the balcony of the hotel we were staying at in Miami. I'll never forget that moment. One of the drug dealers was pointing down to the harbor. "See that building right there? See that boat right there? That's the Feds. And that boat, this is where they bring the stuff in." Everybody was talking about the kind of coke they were getting, where it came from, how much they would make from selling it. This was like a regular business conversation, matter-of-fact.

The thing is, after those Miami nights, every night of touring became like that. On all of our major tours the parties raged; almost everyone got high. The one exception to that was the tours we did with Public Enemy. When we were out with them, they were always nonalcoholic, nonsmoke, allowing none of that stuff in their presence. Only Flavor Flav partied; he drank and smoked with us.

For the next five years, all my nights became like those Miami nights. Even when I came home.

It's hard for the average person to understand. When you're the headliner of a major arena tour, life is like Las Vegas. Money, time, and normal standards of behavior are meaningless. It's sex, drugs, rock 'n' roll, twenty-four hours/seven days.

Maybe it's boredom that causes guys to do these things.

Me, I spent a lot of time and a lot of money on reefer and

drinking. I've done some things that sound bizarre. In fact, they were bizarre. But you've got to understand the type of life you're surrounded by.

That's not to excuse it.

After Run-DMC did our first tour, we learned a lot. We were watching how much the promoters were making on their end, and vowed that wouldn't happen again. We decided that, for our next turn on the road, we were going to run the tour. Run-DMC is going to book the acts, we're going to pay the venue, we're going to arrange for security.

And, of course, we're going to make ourselves some money.

At the end of the night, we'd meet in a room and divide up our take from each show. After all the expenses were accounted for, everyone got their cut. We usually had something like eighty-thousand dollars sitting there on the table in front of us.

The accounting system was very simple. "Okay, here's twenty-five thousand for you, twenty-five thousand for you, and twenty-five thousand for you."

I mean, we're just wadding up piles of bills and handing it out. Ridiculous. And even more ridiculous, all I could think about when I got that money in my hands was how high I was going to get tomorrow. How much cheeba, beer, and food we're going to get with that pile of money.

At that point in my life, when we were selling a lot of records and out on the road constantly touring, it wasn't unusual for me to walk around with fifteen thousand dollars in my pocket.

That kind of money makes you do crazy things aside from the drinking and drugs. In the early days, guys didn't pack their bags for a long trip. It was like, "Oh, we got a tour?" We'd just get on the bus with money and buy underwear, socks, undershirts, T-shirts, and jeans on the road.

After the concert, at the end of the night, we'd just take our clothes off and leave them in the hotel rooms. We didn't have the sense to clean them or hire a valet on the road. It was, "Ooh, my pants stink." And I would ball them up and stuff them in the garbage. I can imagine maids coming in and going, "That's stupid! I can press these and have brand-new pants for my husband and son."

I remember Run having a fur coat and throwing it in the trunk of his car. I mean, this was a fur coat. Didn't matter. He'd get a new one if he needed it.

It's hard to remember how much I ran through spending money foolishly like that. I guess maybe $850,000 slipped through my fingers during those years, when I think of all the reefer and stuff that I bought. Like, there were times where I'd buy a big thing of cocaine just to have it around. You ain't going to sniff all of that. You know what I'm saying? Just to have it around, just in case.

At times, I believe, I was using a lot of this stuff just to calm myself down. You drink a lot, and it becomes second nature, to the point where you wonder how you can go onstage without it.

I remember the first time we're playing Madison Square Garden in New York. I mean, this is the biggest venue in our hometown. We're the headliners.

You know, I was scared to death. *Scared to death.*

We had just played Philadelphia the night before. So we get on the tour bus right after that show. Nobody gets to go home because we got soundcheck that morning. So we drive up from Philly, check into the hotel, and wake up the next morning.

Easy to talk about. I didn't sleep.

I woke up the next morning scared. What if I forget my lyrics? That happens often, but hey, this is my hometown. The rhyme on your record that you rhymed all the time—you get to that point in the song, and it's just like . . . blank. And then Run looks at me, and he's got to pick it up. If I forget my lyric, a lot of times it'll make my partner forget it, and then we got to look at Jay to say, "Where we at in this music?"

A lot of that has to do with what we were doing before the show. Olde English was my beverage of choice during that period of my life. It was such a routine thing. You know what I'm saying? You're drinking beer all day before you do the show.

Anyway, here's the routine: we finish the show in Philly, and we drink beer all the way on the ride back to New York. You get to your hotel, you drink some more beer. Then the sun is coming up. "Yo! It's time to go to bed." You lay down anywhere from 6:00 A.M. to 10:00 A.M.

Then, after only a few hours sleep, you get up. You don't eat breakfast. You're either too high off of cocaine, reefer, and beer, or it's not time to eat because you just went to sleep three hours ago. So you get up, take a shower, put on your fresh gear, and go to soundcheck.

Usually on those sorts of days, we're not feeling great, owing to lack of sleep and what we did the night before, but we're not feeling that bad. Because by the time we get to soundcheck, there's some more beer there for you, and that hair of the dog takes care of any lingering hangover.

So you drink that beer and you do soundcheck like you're doing your concert, and that energizes you back to the point where you're ready for anything. Once you finish that, then it's just about waiting for the show to start. So you head back to the hotel room, where up in the main suite are cases of Olde English and enough reefer, cocaine, and whatever to keep you high until show time.

We used to call it getting pissy, all this constant activity, because if you drink beer all day, you pee all day. The routine is pretty simple: you wake up in the morning, you get pissy all day, you smoke reefer all day, and you eat.

By now, owing to all that drinking, everyone has a big appetite. "Oh, give me three cheeseburgers, two fries." I'll admit we were gluttons, wasting stuff.

But that was what we always did. The same cycle over and over. And over and over.

On the occasion of the Garden show, because the arena was near the hotel, we walked over rather than take a limo. We were so high, we wanted to walk rather than take a limo. You get nervous, you want to be doing something.

You know what door to go into at the Garden because the

road manager has prepared you. "Go down Eighth Avenue and walk down until you see the green awning."

Then, about an hour later, it's on with the show.

Our Garden homecoming was a sold-out show, and it was pandemonium when we walked out onstage. There's just something about Madison Square Garden, a big arena that can feel really intimate. When they flashed the light on the crowd, it felt like you were back up there in the last row with the people. It felt like it was small.

Onstage, I'm towering over all these people. They go "hahhhhhhh." And you just absorb their energy. I'm like, "Oh, wow! This is really cool." It was new, back then.

That was a time when I would go onstage and experience the moment. You don't think about your wife and kids, the bills that you gotta pay. You aren't worried about how you're going to spend the money you're getting that night. It's the show, and you're the center of attention.

Naturally, you come off the stage on that sort of adrenalin high—every seat sold out, totally knocking them dead—and you're ready to party. And you spend a lot of that money you just earned.

That's when the hard lessons kick in. And now that you understand a bit of my history, I'd like to share some of them with you.

Lessons Learned

So, you ask, why am I here?

I've been recording and touring lately. But I've also spent a lot of time on the college lecture circuit, talking to the children of the people who first bought my music. I draw on the lessons I've learned, the mistakes I've made, and the path I've chosen to follow as a result of learning from those mistakes.

Because of my status in the entertainment industry, I can command a lot of attention from groups of people who might not normally tune in to the type of messages I deliver.

But what I tell them applies to all of us, so I thought I'd take the time to drop in on your world and share some hard-won

43

knowledge with you on a topic that is one of the most important things in our life.

I'm talking about respect.

It's a heavy thing. Use it wisely, and it creates goodwill, positive energy, constructive dialogue. Use it in a self-aggrandizing way, and you have confrontation.

Of course, an important part of respect is self-respect, and I've gone through a number of changes in my life in order to understand how important that is.

But the concept reaches beyond self. There's respect for others. Respect for your wife, children, coworkers, bosses, neighbors, friends, job, environment, countrymen.

If you think about it, getting respect, having respect, and showing respect are the forces that make the world work.

The president goes to China, he has to comply with the wishes of the host as a sign of respect.

The gangsta on the street has to be tougher than the next guy in order to win respect. We've all seen how that plays out. Confront and demand respect, and either you'll get it—or the person being challenged will decide to ensure a little respect on their own part.

The businessman? He strives to make more money than the next guy, and those that do are "respected" members of the business community.

To me, respect is about spirit, integrity, and keeping yourself and your business clean. And that's what I want to talk to you about. The right way to get respect. It sounds simple. But as we'll see, it's far from that.

First, you gain respect by reaching outside your own perceptions and actually trying to understand someone. One of the ways we can generate respect is to open our minds and our hearts, looking beyond the first impression.

I'll give you a few examples.

In the beginning of Run-DMC's career, we had no cars. So

we used to take the train to the city when we had to sign contracts and deal with other business stuff. But when we'd get on the train, we'd notice that instantly the older ladies—and some young people too—actually got up and sat down at the other end of the train, far away from where we were sitting or standing. We had just walked through the door of the car, not run in or jumped in. But just showing up was perceived as a threat.

On those same trips, we'd inevitably find ourselves walking across the street in Manhattan. We were wearing our usual uniforms of the day, the same stuff we wore onstage: gold chains, hats, and me with my big glasses.

As we crossed the streets, I'd always hear this percussive noise: "Clunk! Clunk!" Doors locking. "Clunk! Clunk!" Walking across Fifth Avenue in Manhattan, it was like a drumbeat. "Clunk! Clunk! Clunk! Clunk!"

Hey, I understand their caution. To them, we looked like the kind of guys they read about in the newspaper or saw on TV, the worst sort of element. Gold chains, boom boxes, the sort of killer/drug dealer/rapist that's ready to set it off, at least in the TV shows and films of a certain kind.

But you know what? That gear wasn't intended to convey any kind of message. It's just a look the whole neighborhood used to have. And most of us were good guys. Okay, we weren't wearing white hats. But you know what I mean.

If they had only known what we were really about and what we would become, they would have given us respect. Instead, they closed their hearts and minds and believed in the stereotypes.

One of the problems with stereotyping is that those most victimized by it often help reinforce it, maybe as we did when we were wearing our neighborhood outfits. Except now it goes beyond what kind of clothes you're wearing into a presentation of a lifestyle.

There's a lot of rap music, as we all know, that has lyrics that I wouldn't allow my six-year-old son to hear. You know, people who proclaim that they're the newscasters of the ghetto and stuff like that. Which, in their mind, justifies their message, no matter how violent, sexual, or laced with profanity.

But you know what? They're creating a caricature of what they believe life should be like, rather than reporting on what's going on in their lives. It's not like most of them live that way now. Or, in a lot of cases, ever lived that way at all.

A bad excuse a lot of rappers give to justify their violent and obscenity-laced records goes something like this: "Yo, when I'm making these records and when I'm portraying these images, I'm keeping it real. The things that we rap about on our records and the things we put in our videos, it's stuff that we read about in *USA Today* and *Time* magazine every day."

You know the rest of the argument: "Arnold Schwarzenegger shoots people in his movies, Bruce Willis does it. Nobody says anything about what they're doing."

Here's what I tell them in rebuttal: that man is an *ac*-tor. Get it? Acting and rapping are two different things. People have come to realize that a screen actor is portraying a fictional character. But in music, very few of the rappers will admit that they're creating a fictional character.

Let me give you another example of how the image and reality can be really different.

Way back in the day when we were starting out, we did one of the first major rap tours to cross the country. On it were a lot of guys—I won't name the guilty—whose image was clean and positive.

Then we get on the road. It was like they were just living to see how many women they could lay. That disturbed me. When I met all these guys I thought they had a mission, that we were going to use our music and conquer the world and stuff like that.

And it kind of like, you know, hurt a little to find out the truth.

Lessons Learned

Some of my biggest heroes have let me down by not sticking to the truth.

We were doing a show in 1982 with New York radio station WRKS, known as KISS-FM, with Grandmaster Flash and the Furious Five, who we idolized. Me and Run are standing there by the side of the stage, and it's like a dream. I'm getting to see our idols, Grandmaster Flash and the Furious Five, up close and personal. I'm loving every minute of it.

So we're standing there and the show begins. Flash comes out and he does his thing, DJing, no gimmicks. He's really cutting it up. Everybody is going crazy. It's great, it's honest, it's fun. It's real.

Then Melle Mel and the others come out with leather gear and boots and fur and braids, looking like the rock group Kiss. And when I saw that, it was like my jaw just dropped. "What are they doin'? What happened to the sheepskins and the Pumas and the Lee jeans and the mock necks and the gold chains, the stuff from the streets. What are they doin'?"

But it became a trend. Every group that I started seeing, they weren't dressed like what I used to see on the flyers. They got on stage outfits.

We knew that wasn't the way to go. So we decided that we would be dressed like we always dressed when we performed. That's why we said on our record *My Adidas* "We took the beat from the street and put it on TV." That's the honest way. That's the real way.

In the same light, I'd like to call on my fellow performers to honor what they preach. Yes, let's keep it real.

You want to talk about bitches and ho's on a record? Admit that your attitude is helping to create disrespect for women.

You want to talk about violence on the streets? Admit your role in glamorizing it.

You want people to listen to your message and take action? Then deliver an honest message and then live up to it.

———

The tragedy is, some of these rappers don't realize that when they speak, the power of life and death is on their tongue. They are worshiped by impressionable people who take their fictionalized portrayals and turn it into gospel.

Gangsta rap, the rawest version of my art form, is where this power becomes most dangerous. Each guy who came after the originators had to be tougher than the next guy, because they think that by talking about even more violent things, they'll sell more records. It's a never-ending cycle of one-upsmanship.

The artists claim they want to stay true to their roots. "All right. I sold crack. Now I got a record deal. Now I got to keep it real 'cause I remember where I came from."

But what's the point of that? You're better off than you were now that you've got a record deal and a fair amount of celebrity. Yet you're still showing yourself in your videos at parties with loose women. You were doing that when you were selling drugs to earn the rent.

So why not take it to the next level now? Why aren't you giving my son and everyone else any vision, any insight into how you overcame your beginnings? Where's that respect for yourself and your fellow man?

The ultimate realization of that lack of vision comes when we think of the deaths of Tupac Shakur and Biggie Smalls, two rappers gunned down in the prime of life and at the height of fame.

Here's what Biggie said on his first record: "It was all a dream / I used to see Salt 'N Pepa in a limousine / Word Up Magazine." He said, "I want to leave this life of crime and drug selling and move on, to become a rapper and make things better for my family and people in my neighborhood."

And so he did that. At least at first.

His first single and his first video were beautiful. You really felt for this fat black kid from Brooklyn talking about "I'm just hustling to feed my baby, my baby daughter." You felt for that.

But when it was time for him to release his entire album, he got away from that. Now he was talking about the blunts, the AK-47s, the women. Everything that he claimed he was trying to get away from, he was embracing and presenting in his videos, talking about murder, death, I got my rottweiler, I got my laser sight, I got my AKs, back up.

It's not just him. Other rappers claim they want to get away from all that to a better life, then bring those same images and those concepts into their material.

I believe that in Biggie's case, it's the very thing that killed him.

Same thing with Tupac. Same with N.W.A's Eazy-E, who died of AIDS. Everything that's going on in our community that the rappers claim they'd get away from when they made it, they're bringing this stuff into their music, and it catches up to them. It's an endless cycle.

They're trapped by that image. They feel if they give up that image, they'll lose their following. And the sad thing is they don't understand the personal power they have to go in another direction, to be strong and take a stand against the bad things they're describing. We need some strong heroes who'll fight the good fight. That's what's missing in our society, something we've lost along the way.

Two years ago, I saw Tupac's and Biggie's mothers appear at the MTV Video Music Awards. Their ceremonial display and video tribute to their sons set off a celebration that I just shook my head at when I was watching.

With all due respect to the artists and their mothers, I didn't understand the point or the purpose of their appearance. It was like everybody was celebrating the significance of what Tupac's and Biggie's deaths meant, as though they were martyrs to some cause that nobody seemed able to define. Instead, everyone seemed to be advocating some vague "fight the power" notion that was symbolized by their pictures.

Well, I would argue that they spent most of their lives fighting the wrong power.

It's like everybody's rebelling, but for what and to what end?

These guys died. They got killed. The streets are still messed up. And it's a damn shame that they died for the reasons they did, but no one seems ready to acknowledge that.

I'm not putting it on their mothers, but the way that the hip-hop industry and the nation are looking at the situation, they missed the point. Tupac and Biggie died of gun shots borne of foolishness and ignorance. It was stupid. It's nothing but stupidity.

By putting them in the role of sacrificial lambs, the MTV Video Music Awards and those who support it indicate that the party continues. The same atmosphere that led to their deaths is still on. Why couldn't their deaths signal a change?

I wish those mothers had gone up to the podium and helped us all understand the grief they felt by making sure that no one else's mother, father, sister, or brother had to go through it.

If only they had said, "Listen, I want to talk to you seriously. You're all busy out here praising my son. I wish I could have saved him. I did all I could. And the things that he did were his choice. But glorifying Tupac isn't right. The way he went out was a sorry thing. We shouldn't make it Tupac Day."

This should be the day where we look at all the factors that went into Tupac's and Biggie's personalities and deaths, and vow to change things so they never happen again.

Otherwise, the way it stands now, we can only conclude that most people think it's cool to go out like that.

That kind of attitude is why it's important that we challenge everyone to justify their image.

Back in the day, LL Cool J, Run-DMC, the Fat Boys, all of them weren't playing fictional characters. They were themselves.

When we started out, Jam Master Jay was comfortable enough to put a Run-DMC hat on his son and take a picture with him. It was cool and it was cute.

The kid would be holding a gun today. That's what's ruining rap and keeping it in the gutter.

Yes, the music of today is good, and enjoyable if you consider it only as music. But the rest of the message is a disgrace. To an impressionable seven-year-old, listening to songs advocating cars, money, wild women, and the gangsta lifestyle is bending them in the wrong direction. "That's what I got to be," that seven-year-old says. "I gotta be Biggie, I gotta be Tupac. And I gotta be rougher than them."

Hey, I'm not advocating censorship. Lil' Kim can rap her explicitly sexual rhymes. And if my son get his hands on it, he's going to get his hands on it, just like the kid got his hands on his father's *Playboy* book in the sixties. And if someone wants to advocate the violent overthrow of the world, more power to them.

It's when that style becomes the dominant style—the only style in the mainstream—that I get worried. That's why rap is going to keep getting called rap and not simply "music," and why it's in a special "rap" category at the awards shows. It's treated like a documentary film, acknowledged but certainly not honored in the way that feature films are celebrated.

I'll give you an example of that thinking from my own career. In 1986, we were up for an American Music Award against New Edition and Stevie Wonder and Whitney Houston and Anita Baker. There was no such thing as a "rap" category.

I don't know if what happened to us at the ceremony caused the category to be created later, but it might have had something to do with it.

We were the hottest thing on the planet at that time, with our *Raising Hell* album out and rap getting a lot of mainstream attention. So we went into the ceremony sort of counting our chickens before the eggs were hatched, planning on taking home a mantleful of trophies.

We were nominated in five categories, so we began counting awards. All right. If we get three, I get one, you get one. You ready for yours, Jay? Where you going to put it? We already had our speeches ready. We knew. We're all going to get one. Definitely.

Well, we lost.

It got to the fourth award category, and we were slumping in our seats. Lost that. Finally got to the fifth, and we were all holding our breath. New Edition won.

Mike Bivens, leader of New Edition, was gracious at the podium when he was accepting the award. "I know this really belongs to Run-DMC." He knew, even if the voters wouldn't acknowledge rap as an equal category with other forms of music.

Right after that, they started with the rap category. Maybe it was an acknowledgment back then that voters wouldn't accept rap as much as they would mainstream music, so that way, at least some rapper would be honored and not totally shut out from winning a trophy.

But I also wonder—and this is just me thinking out loud—if creating that category at the American Music Awards and the Grammys was really a plan to keep rap in a place where they can keep it under control.

Back then—hell, even today—there are people who think rap is growing too big. This inner-city, youthful, rebellious, so-called black music culture is taking over the world, and that rubs a lot of people the wrong way. They made the rap category and they don't want to let us grow out of it. They don't want us to leave the street corner. They want to keep us there.

Yes, it would be embarrassing to acknowledge a pure rap album as the album of the year. Note I said "pure rap" album. Lauryn Hill won her Best Album Grammy as much for her singing as she did for the rap parts.

If I rap over a rock record, I want the best rock album Grammy. If I rap over R & B, I want best R & B record.

I don't want a rap award. Because then that's just saying the panel that selects the awards, or the entire music industry, is racially oriented and trying to segregate by race.

If you notice, Limp Bizkit, Kid Rock, and all of these new hybrids, they're rapping. But they're looking at it as the new rock and roll. If it was a black group doing it, it would just be rock/rap.

You think I'm being paranoid, that such thinking doesn't exist in our enlightened times? Well, check this out: they're playing Limp Bizkit on all these rock stations that our new record company, Arista, wants to get our records on.

These stations didn't want to know about our records before we recently did the Family Values tour, where we toured with Limp Bizkit. But after we came off the tour, one of our Arista representatives told me that they sent the radio stations playing Limp Bizkit some of our classic rock/rap records, "Rock Box," "King of Rock," and "Walk This Way." He said that we might get played now because of the association.

But if Limp Bizkit never existed, they would keep us as rappers, these black rappers, Hispanic rappers, ghetto rappers, in this rap category. And I don't agree with that.

I want to bring rap to the same level of respect as other music. Put me next to Bruce Springsteen. Don't keep me down here in this segregated area and label me as "just a rapper."

I'm not a rapper. I'm a serious musician-artist.

That's not to say I've been totally righteous about everything I've done in my life or career.

Oh my. We were hypocrites when it came to telling people what to do. And I'm talking about all of us in Run-DMC. We were the golden boys to a lot of people, the shining examples, the rappers who told everybody to stay in school.

Meanwhile, away from the public's eye, we're doing everything that we were warning people against.

Run never really sniffed cocaine, but he was smoking reefer. Jay would get high on reefer and do coke. He soon stopped sniffing but continued to smoke weed. And me, I would do a little of everything. So we're all getting high, drinking like fish, sleeping with women all over the map.

Yet every night it seemed we were on TV, captured from the mayor's program press conference that morning or speaking to kids in schools.

We're telling them that drugs are for losers.

There were so many days that I spent speaking to kids when I didn't know how I got up that morning. Someone would rouse me at ten in the morning and next thing I know, we're going down to city hall and I'm standing there cocained out of my brain and saying, "Don't do it."

I always had big, dark glasses on, so no one could see my eyes. But even on the days when we weren't high, we were drunk. We would sit in the limousine and drink Olde English malt liquor, the forty-ounce bottles, on the way to the drug rally.

We're in the back of the car, Run's rolling a joint, I'm drinking a forty-ounce bottle of Olde English, Jay's getting high on both.

It was ridiculous. Absolutely ridiculous, and an insult to everything we supposedly stood for.

But I still think we were good guys.

Let me explain. This may be hard to grasp for a lot of you, but it's an important distinction.

A good kid is someone who may indulge themselves but doesn't want to harm anybody. Yes, we had our vices, but we're not going to hurt nothing in our attempts to keep the party going. We're not going to rob or stick up anything, draw blood or be violent just to get high. We'd get high, laugh, and be stupid, but that was something we'd always done. We were doing it when we were just kids going to school and doing our chores. We were doing it and remaining mannered and educated and conscious about our community.

It was just a fun thing to do. It didn't hurt our lives, and we weren't pushing anything on anybody.

Because of that stance, we always had an image of ourselves as different than the people who did resort to crime to feed their habits. We felt like we were somehow respectable, that we knew the place of such things in the grand perspective. That's why when we made our early records, we didn't write about some of the things we did in real life. Although we did things that could be construed today as "gangsta" stuff, we felt it wasn't our real nature, a true representation of what we were about. It

54

wasn't what made us *us,* nor was it something we particularly wanted to advocate.

I say that at the risk of sounding like a hypocrite again. Because there were occasions where we did some minor robbing and stealing.

I'd steal money from my mother every three weeks. Yes, I did. Went in that purse and took a few dollars. I didn't do it every day. But I did do it.

And I did rob a stranger. Run recalls it a lot when we're together, reminiscing. He always says, "Yo, D. You was starting to wild."

We think it was a police officer, this white guy we took down. He showed up in the neighborhood and gave us five dollars to go into the reefer house to buy some reefer for him. So we took the five dollars and went in the house, but came out another door around the corner and ran. We said later that the guy had to be a cop. If we had gone in and bought the bag, we'd have come out and they'd have probably gone in and busted the joint.

At least, that's how we justified it.

I also hang my head in shame when I think of the time I used to pick on this fat, snot-nosed kid on my block named Jocko.

Oh, I knew I was picking on him. I deliberately picked on him. I went out of my way to pick on him. And what's bad about it is when I first started doing it, I felt the wrongness, but I kept doing it, and it felt good to do it. I told Run that and he laughed until he cried. 'Cause he knows. He knows 'cause he's had that feeling before.

I did bad things to poor Jocko. And after I was done, he would always threaten me with revenge in the only way he could. He'd say, crying, "I'm going to go tell your mother you smoke reefer!"

That would throw me into a panic, and I'd have to placate Jocko. "No, no. Come here. Come here." Then I'd try to be his friend and wind up bribing him not to go tell my mother I smoked reefer.

Despite all these stunts, we didn't cross that fine line between something that we considered to be at the "prank" level, and some serious stuff, like holding up a gas station or liquor store. That was our mental barrier between respectability and lowlife behavior.

Again, your community probably has different standards. In mine, most folks, particularly the ones around my age, wouldn't think much of it.

A lot of people I went to high school with went a little further. This was in the eighties, when crack became an epidemic. There were a lot of kids going to jail for life—some of them friends of mine.

I remember seeing one guy in particular on TV. I knew him in school. He was a nerd in school and now he's in jail for life. Instead of my friend from high school, now he's the guy accused of running all of the drugs on the south side of town. Was a good kid back then. Was . . .

Look, I'm not trying to excuse our behavior. But we managed to stop ourselves at the crossroads where we might have done something more serious. Our nature was to be good kids and try to get straight A's and stuff like that.

When we started to get a lot of money as our career took off, we were able to keep focused on presenting ourselves as we imagined ourselves to be, even though the real life story may not have been up to that image.

The music industry, believe it or not, probably had a lot to do with saving us. Because we were able to finance our indulgences, it never reached that fork in the road for us where you have to make a decision about how to get the finer things in life.

Even though we did some bad things, the message that was getting out to the public was overwhelmingly positive. That's another proof that music and video and image has a powerful effect on people's lives, for better or for worse.

Now that I've painted a negative picture, let me tell you about one of the better instances.

Lessons Learned

About six months ago, we were in Detroit and a guy called into the radio. It was just me and Jay. Run wasn't there. The guy started telling us what Run-DMC meant to him.

The caller said, "Back in eighty-four, I was illin'. I was gang-banging. I was getting high. I was about to die or end up in jail. But when Run said, 'Stay in school,' because your records were so dope, I went and got my diploma. I went to school and now I'm going to college and I'm going to be a doctor soon."

He's not the only one. We had just played Las Vegas the week before that and a guy came up to us after the show and said, "I was locked down for five years. But your records, your records kept me grounded, dude. Your records made me say, 'When I get out of here, I'm not coming back in here.' "

So, yeah, I look back now and say how hypocritical it was for me to be high and telling kids not to do drugs. I admit that.

But what I was saying was more important than what I was doing, particularly for society. And maybe if enough people keep talking about the right way to do things, it will give people courage to pick themselves up when they fall down and do the right thing.

I remember one day in particular, though, that might have stopped me from going any further along the path toward "rap stardom" that I was heading down. It didn't make me stop indulging myself at that time—that came much later, unfortunately—but it had a profound effect on my attitude about who I really was that lasts to this day.

I had a 1986 Black Fleetwood Cadillac. It had the rims, gold, totally loaded. I loved that car.

My usual routine was to get up in the morning and go to the car wash at Springfield and Linden in Queens, about ten minutes from my home at the time.

On this particular morning, I was really fresh. It was the summer of 1986, and our album *Raising Hell* was all over the radio. I had my new Cadillac. I had new Adidas on. I had a new Adidas sweat suit, a brand new gold chain, new rings on all of my fingers, my Run-DMC hat on, a new pack of cigarettes, a fat bag of weed, a new pack of rolling papers, a new boom box in the backseat, and a pocketful of money.

You get the picture. Life, at least as I knew it then, was sweet.

Bill Adler, our friend and former publicist, used to say the most amazing story ever is how Darryl McDaniels from suburban Hollis, Queens, a straight-A student who went to Catholic school all his life, transformed into "DMC, King of Rock."

Even though I didn't really notice myself going through that transformation, it's inevitable that it will become part of your life. While I never acted bigheaded to anybody around the time we were starting to blow up, I knew what I was doing. You know, I'm putting on my new sneakers, my new Adidas suit, my gold chain, I'm going to get in my Caddy, go get it washed, all these things. I wanted that attention.

This particular car wash is one where you have to leave the car and watch it go through the process. So I paid the cashier and went out in front of the place to wait for my car to arrive.

It's a nice, sunny day, and a lot of people were walking by. Of course, dressed as I am, it doesn't take too long before a couple of people notice me. Soon people started driving by and pointing.

Finally a bunch of young fans approach me, followed by a bunch of older people, and I have a little crowd around me. And they're all asking me for my autograph, talking and joking with me. It's all going fine.

And then I'm looking at them and all of a sudden this feeling came upon me. I don't know what it was, but it was something like dread. I took a good, long look at them and I felt sorry for them because they didn't have what I had.

Some of their clothes were kind of shabby, and it was pretty apparent that some of them were just making it from payday to payday. I looked at some of their sneakers, which were off-brand and really worn, and I just started feeling guilty.

But they seemed so excited to see me, you know? Something's wrong here. You know what I'm saying? I'm here freshly dipped, and there they are, looking like they do, yet carrying on about me.

Then when my car came out, it got worse. "Oh, that's a nice car. Boy, I wish I had that." I heard that from several of them. I felt even worse.

Did it ruin my day? Actually, it ruined the next couple of years for me. I just couldn't shake the feeling from that day, the image I had in my mind of how unfair things could be.

That day in front of the car wash was a wake-up call. The lesson was "No. You don't have to do this. You don't have to be this DMC guy." Since that day, I stopped fronting, which means putting on a false face to the world. I had become this "DMC, King of Rock" guy, but I was trying to carry what I said on the record really far, imagewise. Too far, I realized.

What's really funny is, that same month, Run had the same experience. And since then, that's something we'll always just bring up whenever we feel we're getting too high and mighty.

We can be flying on a plane or we can be sitting in a hotel or we can be waiting to go onstage, and we remind ourselves of who we are. It's something we never forgot from that moment on. We're Darryl, Joe, Jay. Anything else is show business.

You're no better than the next person because you're a celebrity, or because you've got a better job, or because you're more well-off. We're all the same. If you want to be so-called Hollywood, you know, go to Hollywood and do that. Don't come into your own neighborhood and do that.

Living up to your true image explains why Will Smith is doing so well. He's someone who gets it.

How do I explain his success? Number one, he doesn't care what anybody thinks of him. And two, he'd rather take a canoe and paddle the boat himself rather than be a passenger. That's why he started out with "Parents Just Don't Understand" and now comes back with the same style, winning fans both times. It's never been trendy, never been the most popular, the coolest image. But Will has made it work because he lives it.

That's not to say that he likes being Mr. Nice Guy all the time. Will tried one time to slightly alter his image. He had a video: "Boom! Shake the Room." It wasn't violent, but he had on army fatigues and boots and his hook was "Boom! Shake the room!"

And the thing about it was, when he was doing that video, he didn't have a smile on his face. He had that rapper's hard-core snicker. That's not him. He would never make the type of records they were making at the beginning of N.W.A and all of that, but he tried the attitude. It didn't work. He's the good guy, not the gangsta. I think he realized that as well, because he quickly went back to what he does best.

We tried the same thing on our 1991 album, *Back from Hell.* We tried to curse, we're talking about bitches and ho's, getting high, drinking, smacking people with the back of the gun. It was the height of gangsta rap, when N.W.A and Luther Campbell made violence and sex the flavor of the moment.

We made that album out of desperation because we realized our sales were going down, that our appeal was waning. It seemed like it wouldn't be that long before nobody wanted to hear us. Our career slump had also affected our live shows, which provided a good deal of our cash flow. We weren't getting as many shows, and the ones we did weren't paying as much as before.

So we made the choice. We said, "All right, we're going to go make a record that sounds like what the people apparently want to hear."

The album flopped. It might have been what people wanted to hear, but it wasn't what they wanted to hear from us. And because our hearts weren't really in it, it showed. We knew that being gangstas wasn't really us, and so did our fans.

What we decided to do was go back to what made us successful in the first place. We went back on the road for the whole summer, driving in a van pulling a U-Haul behind us with all our equipment. We were getting twenty-five hundred to three thousand dollars a night, way down from the days where we were headlining Madison Square Garden and similar-size arenas, but we didn't care.

We went from town to town, getting back into the sound that we originated, "Rock Box," "King of Rock," just good, live, hard rapping. Doing what we did.

We had to take back the respect. That's why the album that followed, *Down with the King*, was so successful. We were keeping it real.

There's a lesson there for all of us. If you don't do the right thing, and you go the way that everybody else goes, it never seems to work out. It *never* seems to work out.

I think that happens in business and in school and in everyday life. You might say, "Dag, I've been working here eight years and this young guy came in here and after four years he got this position." So your New Year's resolution is to be like him. You wind up getting fired instead. Because the boss knows—and you'll know it soon enough—that certain things work for certain people, but everyone's unique. Try to be something you're not and you'll ruin the good things in yourself.

I regret never having had this conversation with Tupac and Biggie when they were alive. I didn't have time to chase them and say, "Put down the gun, don't smoke the blunt, change your lyrics." I was trying to correct my own problems at the time.

But that's one of the reasons I'm out talking now. I'm trying to live my life by example, and I hope to use my current life— and my past mistakes—as an example.

Everybody who did it Tupac's way is either dead, dying, or in jail or without their careers. And I've been here sixteen years.

Here, of course, is a relative term, given that I've been required to travel the world in the course of my career.

But I've always been a homeboy, and the times I've felt that most acutely is when we went overseas on tours. I've been overseas more times than I can count. Our first trip overseas was to England, right after our single for "King of Rock" came out.

We really didn't know what to expect. When we got over there, they booked us in this old hotel in England. Our road manager, Lyor Cohen, booked us. On the way there, he was hyping it up.

"This is where all the bands stay when they go over here. This is rock 'n' roll, dude. This is a big thing!"

So we were all souped up on the plane going over there. But when we get there, it's like the worst hotel in the world. It was all dirty, dingy, old, really the rock-and-roll routine: liquor, smoke, groupies, dirty linen, holes in the wall. Not a bellman type of hotel.

We were shocked. "We ain't staying here."

They were like, "What's the matter, guys?" It was the hip thing for bands to do, but we weren't buying it.

So we went out and found a better hotel, an upscale place. And that was the last time we ever listened to someone trying to sell us on staying at a "hip" place. From that day, we laid it out: this is how we roll—is the hotel good?

If we find out today the promoter has taken us to some fake hotel, we'll drive around for eight hours going from hotel to hotel to hotel, trying to find one that suits us. It makes the promoter sick, but we always tell them, "This is what you get for not understanding that we want a four- to five-star hotel, first-class seats."

Once we got our hotel situation squared away, it was time for the show. We were playing the famous Hammersmith Ballroom, one of the places where everyone who was anyone played in the U.K.

It was a strange crowd. We never understood why they blow whistles every minute of the performance. You can listen to the live Public Enemy album and hear it; they're still blowing whistles.

Another thing we discovered is that everybody over there drinks beer and liquor and smokes all day. I mean, we did too, but it's like they never stopped. At least we went home for dinner.

Lessons Learned

We was like, "Damn, everywhere we go somebody's smoking!"

Now I understand how they have those soccer fights. They get really drunk over there, but it's a pissy, nasty drunk. We get happy drunk and might have a fight, but they get nasty, sweaty drunk.

That's why it's hard to read their reaction to our music. They were throwing coins at us, everywhere from the balcony to the side seats. And people from the balcony, they pour beer down on you. But I guess it's a happy thing, a celebration.

I guess.

Gradually we came to realize: this is what they do. They blow whistles, they drink beer, they smoke, and they just get bloody, violently, shitty, pissy drunk. It's what they do.

That was England. From there, we went to Germany. Didn't like Germany. I mean, we liked the big cities, Munich and all that stuff, but things like the food . . . we didn't like the food. And again, we didn't like the fact that everybody smoked every minute, everywhere you go.

I guess Japan was my favorite country to visit. Japan was nice. When we finally went to Japan, we got off the plane, and there were people standing there dressed like us. Adidas, Kangol hats, gold chains, Lees. There were maybe three hundred, four hundred people in the airport. It was like some Beatles-type stuff.

That was one of the biggest receptions we've ever gotten.

In Japan, everybody's really nice. Everybody smokes there a lot too, but it wasn't as troublesome. It was like, "Whoa! This is paradise." Yes, Japan felt real good.

One of the reasons were the groupies. I mean, they get attached to you over there. Runny Ray had one groupie that cried when we left, following us to the train station. You really are that sort of unreachable, untouchable, godlike person to them.

Over there, they'll do anything you want them to do. When I first met my wife, she was all full of questions about what my life as a so-called rock star was like, and I was honest with her. So, it was her and her sister on the phone at the same time and they asked me, "Did you ever have two groupies at the same time?"

I said, "Yep, in Japan." When I was in Japan I had two at the same time and they would do anything I wanted them to do. It was pretty simple: we left the club and I was like, "C'mon, you," and they came with me. And when we got to the room, I felt like a Japanese king, because, like I said, they treat you like a god.

That's still true today, and almost more so now that we've been around for a while.

We have our loyals over here, but we got crazy loyals over there. They're like, "Forget Puffy, forget Juvenile, forget Naughty By Nature, forget everybody! Y'all are gods."

Yes, Japan was a very memorable place for me.

One other question my wife and her sister asked me: did you ever date a celebrity?

Well, it depends on your definition. Every time we went to London, there was this veejay on London MTV, a little blond-haired girl, who would interview the band. She was always very friendly and upbeat around us, but nothing particularly forward.

Then about two years go by, and we go to Switzerland. I see her at the show, and we go out together to the after party . . . and then push came to shove, and, yes, I had an interesting time with her. It gave me a lot of points with the crew. A lot.

We've played some strange places in our day. We recently played in a cowboy joint in Texas. They had a big mechanical bull in there, all rodeolike decorations. I didn't think anybody was going to show up, but we were shocked when the place was packed.

Yes, cowboys in there, loving Run-DMC! It was wild. I would say the majority of the draw was Hispanic, with maybe 20 percent of the cowboy regulars in their cowboy hats and the shirts and the jeans and the cowboy boots. Singing and throwing their hands in the air.

Proving once again that there are no barriers in the music. Only in our hearts and minds.

We just went to the Ukraine. I marveled that conditions like this truly exist. Usually we only see it on CNN or I read about it in *Time*.

Lessons Learned

We flew in from Turkey in a jet that the concert promoters sent over from the Ukraine. We thought it was going to be a nice Learjet, something like Donald Trump would ride in.

Well, it looked like a Learjet. But it was real old. I mean, real old.

It wasn't a propeller plane, but I almost thought I'd rather be on one of those than in this jet. It was rusted and the pilot looked shaggy.

It was just, whoa, where are we going in that?

But we have no choice if we want to make the date, so we get on this plane. There were maybe thirty of us packed into maybe a fifteen-seater. People were sitting on turntables and all the equipment. We were just all over this plane. Yeah, I was worried that we were overloading the plane. I was actually scared, but if I was going to go, at least it would be with my boots on. I remember when we loaded up the plane with our bags and equipment, and it did a pop-a-wheelie. The rear of the plane hit the ground and the nose shot up into the air. Now I'm really scared.

We made it, landing in the Ukraine. Coming in over the airport, we could see old wrecked planes, a pothole-filled runway, and all this debris all over the ground.

That was the runway. The airport was worse.

We get off the plane, we go into the airport. It literally looked like a war was fought there. It looked like no one had been there since 1940. Bees buzzing around, litter, cracks in the wall. Go into the bathroom, it was like going into the sewer.

And nobody was in the airport. They told us the airport was closed.

I was, like, closed? This airport is condemned!

We get in the car, a Lincoln Navigator, the finest vehicle the town had, owned by the police. We literally jet through this town, driving on the wrong side of the street into oncoming traffic, going through the area as though we're on an emergency call.

But one thing struck me as we were driving through the street. There was nothing but poverty. People on the side of the road looked like what was going on in Bosnia, or even worse. I mean poor, dirty, no shoes, that stuff you see on Save the Children commercials. We rode for what seemed like fifty miles from the airport, and all around us was poverty.

On one hand it was very depressing. Dang. They gotta live like this. It ain't like we are going to drive into a part of the city and see some luxury areas so we know there's some hope. I saw no luxury there. It's like people say about our country—even those that have it bad most often have a place to sleep and some food.

Watching the street scene, it made me question exactly what we were doing there. We were in town to play some sort of big music festival with a whole bunch of international groups.

Who could afford to go to this? That's what I wanted to know after seeing the street life. But when we got there, there were forty thousand people.

I took a closer look at the crowd, and I had my answer. In every country, in every city, there's that crowd. A certain elite, with wealth or connections. No different when you got to South Beach, L.A., or the Ukraine. Our audience for this evening were the young, college-age kids whose fathers give them everything.

Everyone was dressed up, the girls in their sexy finery and the guys looking GQ'd out, like those movies where everyone goes to the nightclub to hit on women.

Clearly, it was the upper classes of this society that were at the concert. Even the president or prime minister or royal family or whatever they are of the Ukraine were there.

I guess either they were fans of ours, or they hated rap music. Two or three groups were scheduled to follow us. But they got up and left in the middle of our performance.

I have a tough time with the food overseas. It's not like the stuff I'm used to from growing up in Hollis, or even at my own home.

France has always been a particular sore point. The servings are smaller. Everything is cold. They give you a lot of meat, but not the meat you want to eat. It's like a lot of salami and cold cuts.

What is it with this cold cuts stuff? I noticed all over Europe, even for breakfast, it's cold cut platters and just like a lot of cold other stuff.

Then there's the spices they use. Really different.

But the worse meal I ever had in my life was in Japan. It was after a show and I was real hungry, but there weren't a lot of places around our hotel.

Then I saw this particular place. I don't remember the name of it, but it's a popular chain over there. If you ever go to Japan, they're all over the place and they're always open, with an orange billboard with black writing.

This is in the period when I was hardly eating, or eating strangely. I'd go through stages. Once, for the entire three-week tour, my daily meal was an entire loaf of bread with jelly.

On this particular day, I was really hungry and needed something. So I went into this Japanese burger place and I ordered three of their burgers and fries to go. So I get back to my room, turn on the TV, and open it up, ready to enjoy a meal and some entertainment.

I was distracted by what was on TV, so I didn't really look at the hamburger. It's a hamburger, you know? So I bite into this burger and on it is some substance that was far, far, far different than chili. You ever bite into something where the taste just rushes into you? I was immediately aware: this is wrong. I don't know what it is, but this is *wrong*.

That taste just rushed all through my body, and I immediately reacted by spitting it out and hurling it into the garbage. I just sat there after that, not believing what just happened. That was the worst thing I ever ate.

Don't get me wrong. I have the deepest respect for other nations and their cultures, even when it's something that my background and personal food tolerances don't abide.

In fact, going overseas has taught me a lot about our country and my place in it.

We are a strong nation dealing with weaker nations. When I look at our foreign policy, I see parallels to what happens out there on the street and in the office every day. And I think that if we could learn the proper way to deal with others and show respect, we might turn out to have better relationships with other countries, just as we can get along better as individuals by showing respect.

Take the cases where we've bombed a foreign country under the guise of showing them that we won't bow to terrorism.

I think it just made matters worse for us. Just like when someone gets the better of someone else in the street or in the office, now the aggrieved party is going to really want to come down on us because their whole beef is that we are sticking our nose in places that we are not supposed to.

So here you have the case of the big muscle-bound bully—the United States—basically coming in and taking the lunch money of these foreign countries just because they can get away with it.

Yes, there are evil terrorists in those countries, but the majority of people respect America enough to know not to mess with us. But we just came in and even if we killed the bad people, we killed innocent people too. Instead of increasing respect, it makes them less respectful and more eager for revenge.

The key for us is to respond properly. That means constantly, twenty-four/seven, putting the pressure on those that are suspected of being terrorist groups.

Nag them to death! If this is what the Big Dog United States is after, confront them on their own ground. Knock on the door constantly, let them know that they face trouble not only after the fact, but before. That doesn't necessarily mean literally knocking on the door by invading their country. That means constantly beating the drums and having dialogue on whether we can search suspected areas.

Lessons Learned

I think the United Nations incident where we wanted to inspect Iraq for suspected weapons is a classic case. We forced other nations to side with them because big old noisy, forceful, pushy America was perceived as threatening them with bombing.

It forced a lot of diplomats into saying they don't agree with the thing that America is trying to do with air strikes, instead of focusing on the real problem, the lack of cooperation by Iraq. That's not the way to go about it.

I think the only time you go for your gun is when they pull out their gun and you can see it. That's the way it works on the streets.

I haven't been discriminated against overseas, but there are subtle things that go on.

Like when I am checking into a hotel. It seems like all the working people in Europe are really mean. All the people behind the desk were really mean to me and I was trying to figure out why. I thought about this while we were on tour in Europe and Turkey for three months straight.

Is it a race thing? I mean, this lady in the restaurant was really mean to me because I was trying to get my eggs cooked a certain way, over easy. The attitude was like, you take it like it is! I want my water without bubbles, they get pissed off! You got to cook my bacon more, they get pissed off. Can I inquire what size the rooms are? Take it or leave it.

Maybe it's a communications barrier. I remember one of the tour guides seemed not to understand me. I told him I wanted to go to the supermarket to get a loaf of bread and some jelly. So we drove on a bus, and he told the bus driver to stop. We got off and he took me into a pub and showed me sandwiches and said, "Bread and sandwich."

I was like, maybe he doesn't understand, so I explained that I wanted to purchase my bread and jelly and make a sandwich later. He said, "No, you take this sandwich." I said, "No, I don't want that." We went back and forth and he's getting more and more angry. It's almost like if I asked for tea, he would give me some hot water and put some sugar in it and say, "Drink!"

Eventually we left the pub and passed a store. I went in and showed him that I had wanted to purchase something. It was like a lightbulb went off for him. He finally understood.

I'm trying to understand this attitude. I think it wasn't because I'm black. It's more cultural, economic factors. I'm this rich American musician. They probably have a little bit of resentment over that. So any misunderstandings or difficulties get magnified. They are frustrated with themselves, not me, but I'm an easy target because of what I represent.

In a lot of those situations, I had to take a step back and analyze that. I mean, it was frustrating for me when I was hungry and someone was insisting I eat the sandwich in the pub instead of buying bread and jelly to take back to my room. But getting angry in that situation wouldn't have gotten me what I wanted.

The point is that what you are within yourself can manifest itself in the behavior surrounding you. If you are angry, arrogant, or unfriendly, you will manifest anger, arrogance, unfriendliness. If you are compassionate, understanding, and considerate, you can usually expect that in return.

I think I can get a Ku Klux Klan man to really like me. I think that. I don't know if that's spiritual or anything, but it's what I believe.

You know, as much as I have had confrontations—the type everyone has in their day-to-day life—I feel I have never been discriminated against. Nobody has ever called me nigger or anything like that. I've never felt that sort of hate.

I've been blessed in that regard. The places I've been and the people I've met have always brought more pleasure than pain. Let me tell you about a few of my more famous friends.

My Famous Friends

One of the best things about being a celebrity is that you get to meet a lot of people that you wouldn't ordinarily meet, see things you wouldn't ordinarily see, do things the average person can only dream about.

Early in my career, I discovered how much fun it could be to get out and actually meet some of the people that I had listened to for years on records or watched on television.

In fact, it was a measure of how successful Run-DMC was becoming when we started to appear with a lot of people that I never thought I'd meet.

On our first dates, we would go on the road and tour with

the early funk bands, groups like Con-func-tion, the Gap Band, and Parliament-Funkadelic. We did a show with Marvin Gaye and with Kool and the Gang. Here we were, on the road with bands whose records were huge just a summer before we hooked up with them.

I never even thought I would see the Gap Band in person. Now I finally came to realize what all those little 45s that my older brother, Alford, was buying were all about, because here I am, onstage with their creators. That's when I realized that Run-DMC and rap in general was something big.

One of my biggest kicks was the time we went on *Soul Train*. As a little kid, I was riveted by all the heroes of soul I first saw on this show. Marvin Gaye, Stevie Wonder, the Jackson 5. Now, I'm grown-up. Here I am at this place. It's me that some little kid is going to be watching on TV.

Performing on the show turned out to be a strange experience, though. There are things that happen in the course of TV production that you don't know happen until you see them up close and personal.

For instance, it bugged me how young the dancers looked. When I was a little kid, they looked so old! But when I got there, it was like, "Dag! They're younger than me!"

And, of course, it was a trip seeing Don Cornelius in the flesh. It was surreal, like I'm not seeing a person, but here's that thing, that famous thing, like I'm looking at the Eiffel Tower.

We met him before the show. He walked up to us with his greasy Jheri curls, that bass voice as deep as a well. "Hey guys. How y'all doing?" I can still hear that and remember the moment. Dag! Here we are, looking at Don Cornelius. We're looking through the makeup, checking to see how old he is, whether his real-life self looks like it does on TV. This is ill!

One crushing blow was laid on us before we got there. It's a secret kept from the public, but *Soul Train* requires all of its artists to lip-synch their performances because of various television union contracts.

We were worried that lip-synching would make us look fake

and would take away from the energy of our performance. But we so badly wanted to do something unique for this show that we had watched all our lives, that we came up with a way around the restrictions. We took our track to a recording studio before we went out there and did overdubs of various chants. "Throw your hands in the air!" That sort of thing.

Anywhere there was a break in the record, we'd bust in with a chant that made it seem like we were performing live. It worked. People who knew us and saw us on the show never knew that we were performing to a tape.

The performance seemed to breeze by, and then it was time for Don to make the obligatory walk over to us for some small talk, that kind of moment where everyone awkwardly stands there as Don's cough-syrup voice drawls out some innocuous question. I remember that it seemed like he didn't know what to ask us.

The main thing he knew was "One of you is Russell's brother. Uh. . . ." It didn't get much beyond that. But then he quickly bridged to "Can you guys come back and do another number for us?"

When we left there, we were bugging on him. "He didn't know nothing! What's up with him?"

Still, I'll always cherish that moment. At least I got to spend some time with one of my childhood heroes. Not like another famous person I had always wanted to meet, but missed my opportunity to get to know better.

I used to love Sade. It was an open secret among my friends.

She had a song called "The Quiet Storm," and in all my rhymes, I used to brag, "When I perform, I'm the quiet storm." That's because I never used to talk, so that's what the guys used to call me in every interview. "He's the quiet storm."

Then Sade came out with the record "The Quiet Storm."

I don't know about any connection there. But then it seemed like something was going on when she came out with the record, "Your Love Is King." I was the King of Rock in our song of the same name. The guys wouldn't let me pass it by, and I played along.

I was like, "That's my girl! She's singing about me!"

Will Smith will tell you. Back when he was just starting in the record business, he and his partner, Charlie, were kind of in awe of Run-DMC. He told me later that the most incredible thing for him was the time he and Charlie Mac were in the next room when we were on tour together.

They got on the phone to one of their moms and told her in a hushed voice, "Mom, we're next to DMC's room." At that moment, I opened the door to the connecting rooms, and told them they could come in and out whenever they wanted. And they were on the phone in the corner saying, "We're next to Run-DMC."

But back to Sade. It was my birthday one year when we were out on tour with Will. So they went to the record store and bought me all of Sade's albums and actually took the displays, every poster and every cardboard cutout of Sade.

Then they knocked on my door and presented me with the next best thing to the real thing.

Sadly, I never did get to meet her. I could have met her one year at the Grammys, but I punked out. It just goes to show you that you never get too famous to feel like you're back in sixth grade.

We were in the audience at the Grammys as nominees. We knew that Sade was presenting an award that night. The guys were ready to pounce.

When she came onstage, Joe and Jay and Russell and everybody with us were looking at me and laughing, smacking me on the shoulder. I didn't feel it, but they said I broke out in a sweat. Later I found out I was soaked.

They're teasing me, but I'm trying to be the composed and dignified member of our entourage. But they wouldn't stop. If anything, my refusal to acknowledge them made them go on more.

Finally Jay actually stood up in the middle of the ceremony.

"D, there she go! D!!" You know, all loud? And people were looking, wondering what was going on.

"There she is!"

Yes, I should have gone up to her later that night when we were both backstage. But I played like the guy with the crush on the teacher. "I ain't going. No. Get off me. I ain't playing."

You know? I just punked out. So if you're reading this, Sade . . . only kidding. I'm married.

Rick Rubin is one of my favorite people in the record business. He's a guy you might have seen on MTV—big, with a bushy black beard, always wears sunglasses, even at night. He's one of the best record producers in the business, having worked with us, the Red Hot Chili Peppers, LL Cool J, Jane's Addiction, and a long list of other huge names.

I first met Rick in his dorm room at New York University. Russell and I used to hang out together, forgetting the business and just having fun. Run would head home, and we'd hang.

We'd head up to Rick's dorm room to get high, sit around, and just do all sorts of things. He had every record, all the crazy movies, all the newest punk rock music. It was fun going over there. It was like going over my crazy big brother's high-school friend's house, where just everything was outrageous.

He and Russell had just hooked up to form Def Jam Records, working out of Rick's dorm room. It was an odd marriage on the surface—this white Jewish kid from Long Island, son of a successful furniture store owner, and a black, street-smart guy from Hollis, Queens. But it was a partnership that shared a vision. Both Rick and Russell were adventurous, innovative, and creative. The difference was that while Rick was that way for the hell of it, Russell was focused on how they could get paid for being that way. Russell would go, "Well, we can capitalize on this. We can get paid with this. We can be the next movement in hip-hop."

Rick was just like, whatever. He was just doing it because he liked what he was doing, not for any particular end. That's why he's rich today. Rick was always encouraging people to do what they felt, not what they thought they should do.

He had an instinct for what's real. Rick would say, "Don't do the watered-down thing. Do the real thing, the thing that's coming from your heart."

Making records became fun once Rick Rubin came on board our team. That's why our biggest-selling album, *Raising Hell,* was so good. The rhymes that I would do in the alleyway while we was beating on the wall, the rhymes that we would do up in the attic just goofing around, that was what Rick captured and put on the records.

I remember being up in that dorm room listening to a demo tape that Rick had gotten from somewhere. He was like, "Listen to this? This guy, he's from Farmer's, right over by you. You know him?"

The tape was from a sixteen-year-old whose stage name was LL Cool J, an abbreviation for Ladies Love Cool James. When I heard it, I was like, "Whoa! Queens got some flava up there!"

I almost died up in Rick Rubin's room, though. We were sitting around listening to records and eating pizza. To this day, I don't know what was in this particular pie. But after having a slice, the glands under my tongue swelled up, and I thought I was going to die.

Rick was like, "No. That's just an allergic reaction to something that was in the pizza, the peppers or something."

But I was thinking I was going to die! "No! I'm leaving!" I'm getting all panicked. And he's like, "Calm down. It'll go away."

This went on for like fifteen minutes. Finally I left the dorm room and went downstairs, outside by Washington Square Park, thinking that the night air would somehow bring me back.

He came and got me. And he calmed me down, and finally I took his advice and just waited. And sure enough, the glands went down.

He probably won't remember that, but I remember it clearly.

So thanks, Rick, for saving my life. And next time, please order from a more expensive pizza place.

LL Cool J became one of my best celebrity friends. I spent a lot of time with him on the road, to the point where it seemed like we toured with him forever.

Run and LL would fight every night, though. LL Cool J was a threat to Run's throne. And when he got real hot, it got to the point where he would come out and steal Run's line—LL would come out and say, "Who's house is this?" And the crowd would say, "Run's house!"

But since LL was the new hot cat coming up, Run felt threatened by that. Run would run into the dressing room and get in his face. "Don't say you're from Hollis! You ain't from motherfucking Hollis! And stop saying your house! This is my tour!"

Eventually it extended beyond words. Our bodyguards and his bodyguards used to fight, his crew and our crew used to fight. Even LL and Jay looked like they were going to fight one night. Hurricane, who used to DJ for the Beastie Boys, was our bodyguard at the time LL was touring with us. He punched LL's road manager in the face.

I mean, it was crazy.

I didn't take sides. I spent a lot of nights just hanging out with LL. He was a quiet guy, really intelligent, and thoughtful about things. I could relate to that, particularly given the chaos that was flowing around us on the tour.

The quiet, intelligent guys were the ones I spent many nights hanging out with on the tours. Jalil from Whodini was one, Doug E. Fresh was another. Even today, there's just something spiritual about him, and I can relate to that. He's been in hip-hop way before me, but he's still here too. He's also the only guy that we worry about when we have to follow him onstage. Because that man does what it takes three of us in Run-DMC to do. He does that by himself.

All of these people are famous, but we're not hanging out together because we enjoy hanging around each other as famous people. It's more than proximity that brings us together. Everybody that I became friends with in this business are people that I would have been friends with if we weren't in the business.

That's sometimes surprising, because you meet a lot of people in the entertainment business, and most of it ends when the tour ends. When I met LL, we used to talk on the road a lot, but I never thought he would come to my home. I was wrong.

The first time he bought his red Audi, he came to my house and pulled up in front and started beeping the horn and yelling, "D! Yo, look at my car!"

That's friendship. That's real.

Of course, everyone wants to know about Run-DMC's most famous celebrity friends, Aerosmith.

We got along fine with them during the recording of "Walk This Way." It was afterward that we ran into some problems.

A few years before, the band's original members had drifted away and record sales had slumped, but they kicked their drug habits, brought back the original members, and with "Walk This Way" reinvented themselves as a pop music band. They once again became a major draw on the concert circuit.

But everywhere they'd go, I know they were hearing the same question we were getting, and they probably get it to this day. "Is it true Run-DMC brought you back?"

When we hooked up with them to remake "Walk This Way," their career hadn't yet returned to its past glory. But shortly after that they took off again.

I don't know how such questions affected Steve Tyler (Aerosmith's vocalist) and Joe Perry (their guitarist) personally, because they're easygoing guys. They probably can laugh off any thoughts that they needed us to come back. But the record company, their marketing and promotions people and publicists, were really upset by that question and took it out on us in a subtle way.

My Famous Friends

When we did our greatest hits album, we asked if we could use a picture of us with them taken during the video shoot. The answer was quick: no. They didn't want any association with us.

Rick Rubin, who used to be Russell Simmons's partner in Def Jam and is a well-known record producer, put the Aerosmith session together. Originally, me and Jay were up at Rick's studio, trying to arrange a song based on just the beats from "Walk This Way," sampling the original.

Rick walked in and asked if we knew whose record it was.

"Noooo. Poison Ivy?" We thought that was the group's name, for some reason.

"No, no. That was Aerosmith."

Rick went on about how we didn't know how big they are and how dope and boom/bang. Finally he said, "It would be real cool if you do a remake of 'Walk This Way.' "

We thought he meant rearrangement, like we were working on. Wrong.

"No. Do a remake and learn the lyrics." That's Rick Rubin, a guy with an appreciation for the classics and keeping it real. "Learn the lyrics. Take the lyrics home and learn them."

Jay thought that was the greatest idea.

I didn't. Cover songs? I said to Jay, "You know, they're trying to ruin us."

But I went along with the program. So I take the tape home and we listen to Steve and Joe's lyrics. I get a pen and pad and we're in my basement, just like the old days, trying to put together something unique.

"Backseat lover. . . ." At that time, we didn't know what Steve was singing. We were like dissing him so bad because the song jumbles a lot of the lines together. We came up with all sorts of weird interpretations, but wrote the lyrics to the best of our ability, and then went in the studio and laid them down. I mean, we just laid it down and left the studio. Job done.

Boom/bang.

The next morning, Jay called. "You got to come back and do the lyrics over."

"No, we did them. What do you mean? We did them."

"Well, now you got to come back and do it over the right way. Rick says Aerosmith is going to be here."

So we all came back to the studio, and over that Saturday and Sunday, Aerosmith did indeed come over.

I'll never forget that session. Steve and Joe are fun to work with, and there was this sort of energy in the air. Don't forget, in those days rock was rock and rap was rap. This was a real crossover project.

Jay was showing Steve and Joe what we did with the record, how we used to rap over it out in the park.

Steve was into it, but he was a bit perplexed about our version. It didn't have any of his vocals. "So," he asked, "when are you going to hear me?"

"That's the key, Steve," I said, kidding him. "You don't get to hear your voice. As soon as the guitar riff gets ready to enter and you come on, Jay mixes back into the drum beat."

He thought that was amusing. But, as you all know, that's not how we did the remix of that record.

By having Steve and Joe there in the room, it made it into a whole new record. There was a lot of energy and fun flowing through that studio.

"Backseat lover / and it's always undercover. . . ." When we were recording it, we sort of improvised it on the fly, how we were going to do the vocals. That's what made it fun. "I take the first lyric, you take the second, yeah, I'll take the third, and we out."

I realized Jay and me had been doing the song with hardly any energy. But when Steve and Joe were there, with all the laughing going on, Joe Perry playing the guitar, doing his overdubs, Jay scratching, we were really getting into this thing, and it seemed to explode.

And by the time the reefer and the beer and everything went around, it was really getting off. "C'mon, Joe. Let's go. You go on that side, I'm here. Yeah."

(I should point out that the reefer and the beer and whatnot

The house where I grew up in Hollis, Queens, NY, 1964–1987. We moved to Long Island in 1987, right after the *Raising Hell* tour.

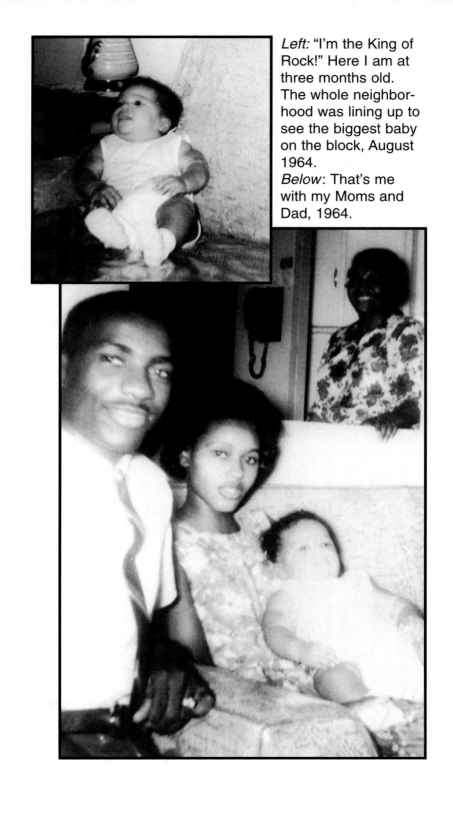

Left: "I'm the King of Rock!" Here I am at three months old. The whole neighborhood was lining up to see the biggest baby on the block, August 1964.
Below: That's me with my Moms and Dad, 1964.

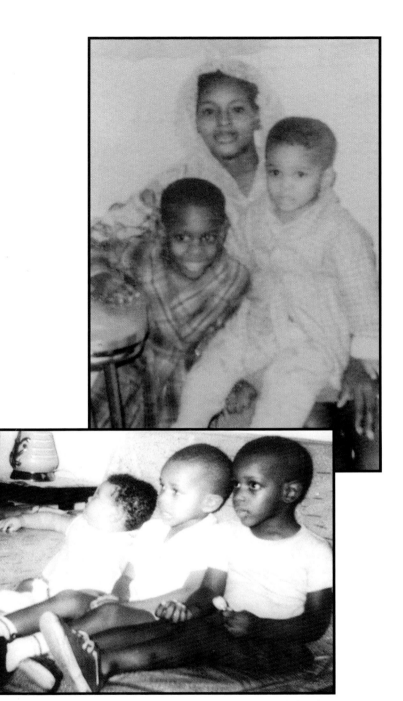

Above: That's me on my Moms's lap with brother Alford (on left) at Christmas, 1965.
Below: "3 the Hard Way." That's (left to right) me, cousin Donnie, and brother Alford, 1964.

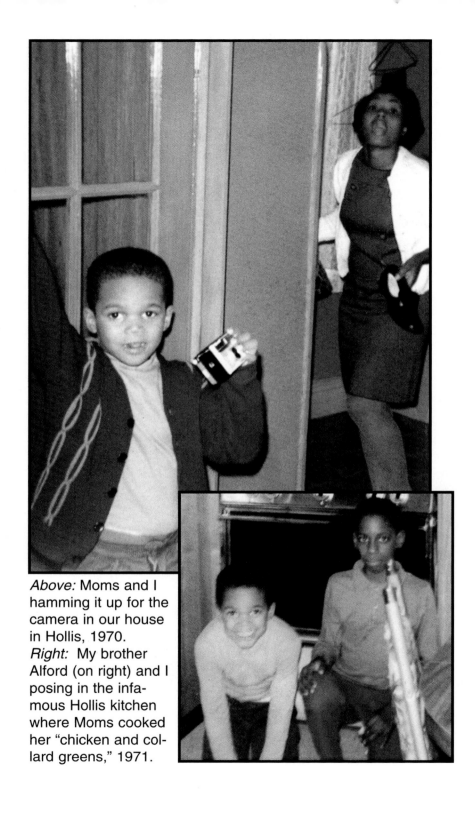

Above: Moms and I hamming it up for the camera in our house in Hollis, 1970.
Right: My brother Alford (on right) and I posing in the infamous Hollis kitchen where Moms cooked her "chicken and collard greens," 1971.

School Days
Top left: Kindergarten
graduation, 1970.
Top right: First grade, 1970–71.
Above: Second grade, 1971–72.
Right: Third grade, 1972–73.

Those special celebrations!
My parents were so proud!
Top left: Sixth grade
graduation, 1976.
Top right: Seventh grade
Confirmation, 1977.
Above: Eighth grade
graduation, 1978.
Right: High school
graduation, 1982.

Top: Moms and Dad, always the happy couple, 1972.
Center: "Moms took this one." That's me, Dad, and brother Alford, 1976. *Bottom:* "Dad took this one." That's me and Alford clowning with Moms, 1979.

Above: One incredible night at the Garden (Madison Square Garden, NYC, Run-DMC/*Raising Hell* tour, 1986) and then I had to walk back to my hotel room!
Right: Performing with Run-DMC, Memphis,1988, *Tougher Than Leather* tour.

Above: In 1988 (back before I almost died from alcohol poisoning). Look at Jay's pants! *Left:* Look! No Adidas! Out on the town with Eric Blam and Butter Love in 1989.

Right: Chillin' with Q-Tip in 1989. *Below:* Visiting Mike Tyson in jail during the Run-DMC *Down with the King* tour, 1992.

Right: That's me with my Moms in front of my parents' Long Island house. I had just flown in that morning from the *Tougher Than Leather* tour to attend my brother Alford's wedding, 1988.
Below: On the road with Run-DMC, *Back from Hell* tour, 1990: (left to right) Jam Master Jay, Run, and me, with Jay's son, Jason, out front.

Above: Here I am, the proud papa, with my son, Dson, just before his first birthday, 1995. *Right:* Dson's kindergarten class photo, June 2000.

Above: Happy birthday, Zuri! January 25, 1998. *Below:* Zuri and I on our way to a *Source* magazine party, 1998.

Above: The Special Olympics, 1995, backstage with Arnold Schwarzenegger: (left to right) me, Arnold, Dson, Zuri, and my mother-in-law, Lauren. *Below:* Backstage with Run after performing for the kids at Great Adventure, 1996.

Above: Steven Tyler and I "Walk This Way" on stage at the House of Blues, LA, 1998. *Below:* Backstage at MTV's Video Music Awards after an incredible performance by Kid Rock, Aerosmith, and Run-DMC, September 9, 1999: (left to right) me, Joe Perry, Kid Rock, Jam Master Jay, Run, and Steven Tyler.

Above: "A Very Special Christmas 1998." Backstage with Sheryl Crow after performing at the White House for the President and Mrs. Clinton. (Sheryl doesn't know it yet, but she's going to make a record with me.) *Below:* Having the honor of meeting Terry Callier, a wonderful soul and great musician, backstage at the Bottom Line, NYC, April 2000.

that was going around was on our side. Steve and Joe were clean, and stayed that way throughout the whole session).

Of course, the fun that we had that weekend translated into the video later on. And, of course, the new version of "Walk This Way" became *the* crossover bridge between rock and rap, a song that will forever be known as one of the key moments in the history of rock 'n' roll.

When we started really blowing up as a group, Russell Simmons started having the cash flow to put all of his ambitions into action. And one of them was to take Run-DMC from records to films.

One night in 1985 I was home in Hollis, Queens, and I think it was about two in the morning, and the doorbell rings. It's Russell and George Jackson, the film producer who later headed Motown Records, and some other guy.

They're all excited, bugging out with enthusiasm, saying, "Yo! We're gonna do this movie. You gotta sign here. We'll be starting in three months."

I had a hunch that a lot of this deal had been made up earlier that night, as Russell and George careened around the city. There hadn't been too much talk about us making a movie. But we were at the peak of our career, and I guess George Jackson was probably looking at how successful the music was becoming, and figured that he could make a quick film that would make some money. So I signed that night.

That was the start of my movie career. The rest of it would follow in similar fashion.

We were really rushed because we was getting ready to go out on the *Raising Hell* tour, which would eat up months and months of our time, far too much to have a coherent schedule for shooting a movie, what with all the promotional visits to radio and publicity and soundchecks.

It seemed like I signed the contract, then I looked up and we were doing this movie, *Krush Groove*. The film was conceived as an update of two earlier films, *Beat Street* and *Wild Style,* both of which showed the early history of rap music, how and where it emerged.

Because we were rushed, there are some people who feel *Krush Groove* is kind of a throwaway film. The plot centered around a struggling record company that's trying to help hip-hop grab a toehold.

A lot of the older white critics just didn't get it, saying that it had no plot. You can see some really bitter reviews out there. But amazingly, none of it had much to do with us. They blamed the filmmakers rather than the performers.

We were the stars of the film, joined by the Fat Boys (who can make you laugh just by walking in the door), Kurtis Blow, LL Cool J, New Edition, and Sheila E., who at the time was Prince's number one protégée. We got lucky on one of the stars of the film. We hired young Blair Underwood, who later went on to fame as one of the lawyers on *L.A. Law.*

Although the critics weren't going wild, the fans ate it up. The film was directed by Michael Schultz, who did the similarly scorned but beloved by fans *Car Wash,* a popular black comedy from the 1970s. The fans appreciated the positive message the film delivered about making it in tough times.

For me, making the movie was easy. I had to play myself and act like I did in real life. They didn't write too many parts for me, and I was kind of glad about that, because I wasn't too sure about this acting business. Back then, I wanted to be true, as close to real life as possible.

I told them not to write any lines that I wouldn't say, don't have me dressing or acting any way other than how I am. I wanted to stay in line with how people thought of me as DMC on the records and in real life.

So every scene had me either rapping or sitting there writing rhymes, which was pretty accurate for what I did in real life. And they made Run the raunchy, energetic kid eager for fame by any means, which he was in real life.

It took a couple months to shoot the film, and the last day of the shoot, we got on the plane to start the tour. It was quite a transition. Making films is a slow, lazy process. I just had to show up and sit there all day, say a few lines, then go home at night. It reminded me of making a record.

But it was a period of relaxation in our hectic lives, so I did enjoy it. One of the perks I really got off on was the new wardrobe. I was getting new Adidas suits, new Kangols, new Lee jeans. I show up, they give me the stuff, I get to keep it.

Because *Krush Groove* was really successful, we got a little more ambitious, particularly as we blew up into one of the biggest groups in the world.

Rick Rubin and Russell, who were partners in Def Jam, came up with the idea for another film based around the urban culture that spawned hip-hop: *Tougher than Leather.*

The plot centered around us, a hot rap group. A small-time music booking agency signs us, but their real purpose is to launder drug money. A close friend of the group's stumbles onto the operation and is murdered. So we take justice into our own hands.

Rick Rubin directed the film, and it starred Richard Edson, Jenny Lumet, Run-DMC, Slick Rick, and the Beastie Boys. It was supposed to be somewhat like those blaxploitation films like *Shaft* and *Superfly* combined with Sergio Leone's spaghetti western films, those ones where Clint Eastwood would ride in, clean up the town, then grimace and ride off.

My verdict: it was retarded. Really retarded.

We should have paid more attention to Clint Eastwood. He once said in one of those Dirty Harry movies that a man's gotta know his limitations, and I'll confess, we probably exceeded ours when we decided to do this film ourselves. We had already been successful staging our own tours, eliminating the concert promoters as middlemen and reaping big financial rewards for ourselves.

So, logic dictates, when it comes time to make a film, we can do the same thing and make even more money.

I've got to admit, it was exciting. We were all thinking, "Dag, we're going to be making more money than we did when we promoted the Fresh Fest tours ourselves. We'll just do this movie the way we make our records. And since we control it, we'll be able to say what we want and shoot, and also put some real Hollis stuff in there."

At least, that's what I thought. But that wasn't the case.

Russell wanted to keep our images intact as the good guys of rap. Even though our music and image was really street, B-boys from the streets, no laces, black leather suits, he didn't allow us to be the real Hollis guys that we hung out with on the corner. No violence, sex, or drugs in the movie.

They completely watered down the dialogue. When we pull out some guns, they had us using lines like, "Oh, these are my grandfather's guns from World War II," instead of "I went down to the corner and bought these guns from PJ and we gonna go out there and find the crack dealers."

You know, it was all just really corny. And it was like the worst experience of our lives.

We had based our whole music career on being real. We wouldn't do nothing if we thought it was fake. But here we are, going through the motions hoping for success. And the end result showed.

Things got so messed up, we ran over our production funds. So we took money we made as Run-DMC and reshot some scenes, hoping we could make the film better.

We couldn't. Today, the movie is viewed as kind of campy, a B movie of the early days of hip-hop that some people feel is something they have to have in their collections. But it wasn't a box office smash, and it pretty much marked the end of our movie career.

It hasn't soured me on a film career. I'm actually looking into getting a cartoon show produced based on my concept of hip-hop superheroes. I loved to draw as a kid, and I have a lot of ideas on paper. I also want to write scripts. I definitely want to direct.

But this time, I want to do it my way. Truthfully.

My Famous Friends

My lack of knowledge on Aerosmith aside, I did grow up listening to a lot of music you might not have expected me to listen to. I was a big fan of New York radio station WABC AM when I was little. A lot of my music knowledge comes from there.

Elton John, "Bennie and the Jets." Stevie Wonder. Harry Chapin.

See, my brother was a little older. He was buying the Ohio Players; Earth, Wind and Fire; and all of that sort of seventies soul. But I wasn't buying records at that time, so I was listening to the radio trying to find Elton John. I used to love Elton John. And Three Dog Night, Black Sabbath.

But my favorite group of all time? The Beatles.

Because my group is like the Beatles. I can relate to what they went through. The start of the pandemonium we created and they created. It's like our stories are so identical, even at this point that I'm at now.

One day I was just sitting at home and was catching a John Lennon biography on TV. They were interviewing the managers and all the other players in that scene.

But then John Lennon was saying, "We tried to come together and collaborate and make the music, but it was just not clicking. We kept trying to do it, and everybody's commenting, and we knew we were faking it. Then it came to a point where we had to admit that it's not going to click. It's never going to be the same because our thoughts and our emotions are not the same."

I could relate to that. I'm married now, with a kid. We're thinking different things now. We're old guys trying to make music for young people.

And that search for something new to say almost led us to one of the biggest mistakes of our career.

We reached a point in our career where we had lost our momentum. It happens to every group eventually. The public tires of you, styles change, your interests change, new faces come on the scene.

By the early 1990s, we were at that point.

So we were looking for someone who could bring us back to the top of the heap, someone who seemingly had his finger on the pulse of what was going on in the rap scene.

At the time we were looking, that man was Marion "Suge" Knight, head of Death Row Records, one of gangsta rap's—and the record industry's—biggest labels.

Knight was a former football player at University of Nevada, Las Vegas, a mountain of a man at six four and three hundred plus pounds. His roster included Dr. Dre, 2Pac, Snoop Doggy Dogg, Tha Dogg Pound, and a whole lot of other gangsta rappers talking about the hard life.

Suge lived it. He was known to dress in red, which people said was a sign of his affiliation with the Los Angeles street gang the Bloods.

You might have heard on ABC TV's *20/20* about the time he supposedly hung Vanilla Ice out the window of a hotel penthouse in order to get a share of his music publishing rights.

Or maybe you heard about the time his crew visited rapper Eazy-E's office with some lead pipes, trying to get Dre out of his contract with Eazy's Ruthless Records.

Perhaps you heard about the twins people say he beat up. Or that the federal government has allegedly been looking into Death Row's ties to gangs. I'm sure you heard that Suge was driving the car the night Tupac Shakur was gunned down in Las Vegas. Earlier that evening, Suge and Tupac and several other associates had been at a nearby hotel, and they were captured by the hotel's security videos stomping on someone who crossed them.

That incident, by the way, violated Suge's parole for a prior assault. He's now serving time in the men's penal colony at San Luis Obispo in northern California. And the police have reportedly investigated his possible role in the death of Biggie Smalls, who was shot in Los Angeles, culminating rap's long-standing East Coast–West Coast feud.

At the time we met with Suge, things were running red-hot with the East Coast–West Coast feud. This wasn't just rhetoric.

There were guys in the street who seriously hated anyone from outside their hometown, or even outside their neighborhood. The Tupac and Biggie situation was only the most visible part of it.

We felt that Run-DMC was the only group that could have bridged that gap. If we had signed with Suge, it would have unified everybody. It would have said that everything is really all right, it's really about records, music, and MCing. That's why all y'all are in this game. This is what it's about.

We sign with Suge Knight and we're putting out records, it solidifies all the beefs various people had. Everybody shuts up.

Plus, it would have been a better situation for us. He'd have spent money on us. It would have been Hammer time. We'd have put out a bomb-ass album.

Yeah, we were aware of his reputation. Run's joke was, "He's going to smack you, D."

I said, "No, he's not. 'Cause I ain't going to sit that close to him. I'm going to duck!"

Jay, who's lived faster than any of us, had reservations about it, openly and plainly. But I felt that it was going to be okay. People knew our reputation. They wouldn't feel we'd crossed over to the dark side just because of who we were working with.

In fact, I felt maybe we would have changed the way people would have looked at Death Row and Suge Knight. This was Suge's chance to prove to people that whatever he did or people say he did, he could work with an act that had a legitimate track record that wasn't a gangsta rap act. He could prove that he could be legit.

Run-DMC was getting ready to take him into an area he didn't know. He would have met new people, had a different outlook on the industry. And it was like he wanted to be taught. He wanted to be schooled by us.

When we were speaking to him, it looked like he was kind of scared to really deal with us 'cause he knew Russell Simmons's history, he knew what Russell had done in the industry. I'm kind of sitting there thinking, "We going to bring God to this man."

You know, we ain't going to preach the Bible to him. But by

us connecting him, it's going to bring God to his whole situation. By us doing it, it's going to end the East Coast–West Coast talk. It's all good.

But, you know, even as he gave us his hopes and dreams, he would also talk about the stuff he did. "I got women that will do anything for me. I got this, I got that." Basically flashing his street mentality.

That street mentality leads back to something I had often thought about before, that talk about how it's all about the Benjamins. It's my theory that Suge made the kind of records that he did because he was a businessman thinking more about how many records he was going to sell than the harm it's going to do to his artists and others.

In particular it was a mistake to do what he did with Tupac Shakur. Because Tupac's energy and disposition was often like dry brush waiting for a match. Suge came along with the match and some gasoline.

I remember one show we did with Tupac. Before the show, we went to the mall and were walking around, killing time. Everybody in there had hats on, which in a lot of malls isn't allowed, because hats are sometimes construed as "gang attire." But in this case, everybody walking around had a hat on.

So, of course, there was one cop there on duty, standing there all day on his shift, watching the hats go by. And then Tupac walks by, wearing his.

The cop walks up to Tupac and says, "Excuse me, son. Take your hat off." And Tupac just snapped. "Oh, man. Everywhere I go, you always on me!"

"Yo! Chill, Pac."

"No!"

We just couldn't calm him down. He was off about how everyone was always in his face. I thought we'd have to drag him away from there.

My Famous Friends

Conflicts followed him. He just didn't know really how to deal with it. In that case, he could of just said, "Okay. I'll take my hat off." It was no big deal. One guy, out of millions, wasn't going to give him his proper respect.

But as much as he sought that respect, he didn't put himself in the position where people could respect him.

He let his anger and his drive for respect be the quality that defined him. In almost every situation, he made the move out of emotion. Take the time he's being let out of court on bail, facing serious charges related to rape.

Hey, the news teams are going to be there. That's a given. But if you want people to respect you and give you the benefit of the doubt, allow you to be judged innocent until proven guilty, you don't come out of the courthouse and spit at the camera on national TV.

How are you going to ever get somebody to respect you after that? Essentially, he spit in the face of the world.

You get more respect by presenting yourself in a way that opens the door to respect in the first place.

I am not a confrontational guy. But I am a guy that people respect. That doesn't come from me arguing, or looming over people, or threatening.

The way I get respect is by respecting a person for being the way that they are.

If I see somebody doing wrong, I say . . . okay. In a day or two or a week or two, this guy is going to be coming back to me asking for my forgiveness. And it is that understanding that keeps me from firing back.

Somebody bugging you in the workplace? Is the boss pushing? Can't get along with this coworker? It is more important that you stay focused on what you have to do.

Your own self-respect is more important than getting respect from others.

Just give 150 percent, whatever your goal is, and don't let anybody try to sidetrack you.

King of Rock

I was just reading an article about the producer Jermaine Dupree. His father is Mike Mauldin, who is head of black music at Columbia Records.

He told his son you'll get more recognition by working hard and not bragging about it then by asking for people to notice you.

I think it is the quiet, reserved person that's really focused, that knows what he wants to do and what he needs to do, that will get more respect.

It's funny. In his quieter moments, when he was giving respect instead of demanding it, Tupac was as lovable a person as you could ever meet.

Later that night, after the incident at the mall with the policeman and before our show, we had a discussion about who should go on in the headlining slot of the show.

At first, we deferred to Tupac. After all, he was currently hot in the movies and on records. "You're a movie star, you're a sex symbol, we ain't going out there to chump ourselves."

By all rights, the slot was his. But he was too polite. "Nope. I don't care. There will be no show tonight 'cause I ain't going on after the legends."

At that moment, in a selfless, quiet act, he had earned respect.

As it turned out, we decided not to go down that road. For various reasons, we didn't hook up with Suge Knight. And I'm glad we didn't. There were no guarantees that we could have turned him away from the path he was headed down.

After all, you are known by the company you keep. And that brings me to another area of my life I'll share with you.

I'm not big on naming my friends. I think when you name somebody something, when you title them "a friend," it ruins it all.

I have no friends in the music industry. You know what I'm saying? Not in the music industry. By that, though, I don't mean my group, because they're guys I grew up with.

My Famous Friends

Jay is my friend. I mean, I'm not involved with his business, I don't hang with him, but he's been there for me.

But you've got to be your own best friend in the music industry. It's that cold.

It wasn't until after the success we had with the *Tougher than Leather* album in 1987 that I began to pay attention to record industry finances. We were having too much fun before that.

It wasn't anything specific that woke me up. But I kept hearing that we were the hottest thing in the world, except our record company was telling us that we were only selling three or four million records. Now, I didn't really think too much about that. But other people started talking to me, telling me that all the early rock 'n' rollers went through something similar when it came to tallying up the sales.

I can't say what I think on this subject. As a condition for getting our money from Profile Records after the label was sold, we had to sign a release where we can't accuse them of anything.

But what I can say is I don't think anybody in the history of rock 'n' roll has gotten a fair accounting. It's what happened to everybody in the business. Because that's how the business is.

Love and Marriage, Food and Family

I never had a lot of girlfriends when I was growing up.

And to my wife, if you're reading this, I think I hear my son, Dson, crying. Maybe you should check on him.

I remember the first girlfriend I ever had. Well, she wasn't exactly a girlfriend. But we were sort of intimate, if only for a moment.

I was in the third grade, and me and a neighbor, Ava, sort of bonded. She was my age, about ten years old, and we were united by our common status as outcasts to her twin cousins, Denise and Barry.

They were mean. They were three years older than us, a long

stretch at that age, so they thought they were more grown-up than Ava and me.

We were just stupid to them, two stupid, snot-nosed kids. That brought us together.

This one afternoon, I don't even know how it happened, we were holding hands. Without saying anything, we went walking down my driveway and headed to the space in back of the garage, which was located behind my house. There was a fence behind that garage, so it was just a little, little space.

I don't even know what we said once we got back there. But the next thing I know, we're standing there with our pants down, holding hands.

All of a sudden, her aunt walked up. I'll remember that moment forever as the scariest one of my life.

She just started screaming, "Oh my God! Oh my God!"

I was scared, but I couldn't run. It was like I was rooted to the spot, and she basically had me cornered in that little space.

Her aunt was Mrs. Getten, and she already had a reputation on that block. She was feared as someone who brooked no trouble. And now she had caught me with my pants down.

I don't remember anything but being too scared to move, as though I were pinned to the wall. I wasn't even going to move to pull my pants up. I wasn't even aware of Ava.

Finally, after what seemed like several days, but was probably just a few seconds, she walked away, pissed. I pulled up my pants and cautiously looked around the corner. She was gone, and so was Ava.

Nothing ever happened beyond that. For some reason, Mrs. Getten and I never spoke of it again, and she never told my parents. Ava just stopped coming over.

After that day, every time Mrs. Getten saw me, she just looked at me like I was the worst criminal; public enemy number one. And I felt like that little kid caught behind the garage. It was like a bubble would come over my head and she could read my mind. It was like she would look at me and I could read her mind:

"Don't tell me hello and what a nice day it is—let's talk about me catching you behind the garage with your pants down!"

Even as the years passed, she still gave me that look.

But one day, after I became DMC, things finally cleared up. Right before I moved to Long Island from Hollis, she finally said hello to me and told me she was proud of me. I felt like I had graduated! It was like, he's finally made it. He's worth something. He's not a pervert!

That was my first girlfriend. Needless to say, my love life wasn't off to the greatest start.

Ava was really one of the only girlfriends I had growing up. The girls were too busy with the bad boys and basketball players and never paid much attention to the regular guys, the students, the artists.

I've always had a good relationship with women. Even when we were on the road and the relationships weren't all that permanent.

As anyone with a passing interest in the music business knows, live entertainment tends to draw all types of people. Some come to enjoy the show and have a good time with their friends.

Others come to enjoy themselves by having a good time with the performers, both before and after the show. It's the latter that I'll address in this section.

A strange assortment of people show up backstage at our shows.

From freshmen in high school to housewives to college students to secretaries. When I was twenty-two, when we were in the prime of our career, it ran from women a few years younger up to age thirty.

I hate to say it, but there aren't very many innocent people in that crowd. These women know what they are there for. They were there to do it all.

There's some crazy women out there. The type of woman that let you know that the moments you spend together are all about sex and nothing else.

I've seen those kinds of women at practically every show Run-DMC has done throughout its career. The craziest of these crazy women guys call "skeezers," a derogatory term meaning a combination of scurvy and sleazy. As you might imagine from that nickname, these are not people held in high esteem by many of the performers and their crew.

I've seen some things on the road that were pretty wild, from some people that I didn't think were capable of such behavior. There's a certain type of mentality on the road. Guys who seemed to live for a lay. Even among my own group.

I was sitting here all day thinking about who was my first groupie. On the real, to be really, really, really honest, I do not remember. It's crazy. I do not remember. I can remember the little white girl, I think about the Puerto Rican girl . . . but whoever was first doesn't come to me.

As I mentioned previously, I'm usually pretty approachable, so I was the kind of guy that many of the so-called skeezers would come and sit down and talk with for a while.

I don't know. Maybe it was the way my mom taught me to respect women. I'd enjoy talking to all sorts of people too. And, like many people I'd meet on the road in airports, they'd tell me, "You're really nice. You're not like the others." I always got that. "You're not like the others."

Yet as I'm sitting there talking to them, and we're really having an interesting conversation, somebody from some group we were on tour with could just walk over, grab her hand, and she would get up and go with him to wherever.

I wouldn't get mad at her. I would get mildly mad at him for his attitude toward women, but not from the point of, "Yo! You takin' my skeezer."

It was more like, "What are you doing?"

I had my eyes opened real fast. I started seeing other groups' behavior, and it kind of appalled me. Whoa! This is what they do and this is how they live? And it kind of like, you know, hurt a little—you know, that ain't right.

It gets back to what I was saying about how people create images, then live down to them. It works the same way for a lot of the women and other people that we'd meet backstage. They're so excited by being in the presence of a celebrity, so over-stimulated by the adrenalin that flows through the room after a big show, that they don't know how to behave. So, as a consequence, they go over the top with their behavior.

All these guys that make certain records today try to use that atmosphere, falling back on the old so that they're merely reporting on the world. "I'm making a bitch and ho record because there's women out there like that. I've seen them backstage."

But I'm telling this guy to take a good look at himself. The only reason that some people behave like that is because of you. You're the one that's got to accept your part for initiating that sort of behavior.

And I might as well confess now that I wasn't only a spectator. Yes, I always conducted myself as a gentleman. But then there came a time when I transformed and started taking advantage of all the available women. One-night stands. Can't even count the numbers of partners I've had.

I guess it was the peer pressure. Everyone was doing it. And if you don't do it, you ain't down. Just like drugs. It was just the thing to do, the macho thing, the cool thing, the down thing.

It's not unusual in the world of sports and entertainment. I justified it to myself that every rock 'n' roller before me, every funk star, had gone through the same thing.

Yes, it was fun for a while. I thought it was the ideal world. And I didn't think it was wrong because everyone else around me was doing it. There wasn't anyone saying not to do it. In fact, it became a topic of regular conversation. "I got twelve last week." Or, more rarely, "He didn't get any." It wasn't considered normal if you weren't doing it, and it actually became something of a competition.

Once, when we were in L.A. we were staying at the Stouffer's hotel on Century Boulevard. Very nice hotel. Back in the 1980s, every celebrity would stay there. I've seen Michael Jordan in the lobby.

At any rate, during our stay, I met this guy in the hotel bar. The guy looked like one of the light-skinned guys from Bone, Thugs & Harmony, Lazy Bone.

I met people there all the time in the lobby bar. I used to just sit at the bar. As soon as I landed, I would put my bag in my room and sit at the bar all day and just drink, twenty-four/seven.

So I meet this guy; he's just buying me drinks all day, all day, all day. So we develop that sort of relationship, I bring him to the show, I'd tell him what room I was staying in, all that. I wouldn't do this now, but I used to tell anybody where I was at, come in my room, that sort of thing.

Things were cool. But then he called me up the night after the show and he's like, "Yo! I'm downstairs in the limo. It's my sister's birthday. She wants to meet you, so come down and meet her."

That's cool. I think I'm doing him a favor, so I get down there, and sure enough, there's his sister. Very nice looking, almost Asian-shaped eyes. But then my friend goes, "Here," and he gives me a gigantic bag full of cocaine and says, "Take my sister."

I'm like, "What?" Thinking he was kidding. He was definitely drunk. She's definitely drunk. But he says, "I'll be back for you later," and heads off.

Not one to look a gift horse in the mouth, me and this girl go back to my room and we sniff cocaine for a while. Then we have sex all night.

Let me tell you, at the time, this was the greatest day of life. It was like, "Whoa, this is what life is all about!" That's how I looked at it.

Looking back at it, it may not have been his sister, although they looked a lot alike. But I didn't care about the girl. I wanted more of the drugs, and I hooked up with him again from time to time to get some.

Love and Marriage, Food and Family

Los Angeles wasn't the only wild time. Down South, early in our career, it was like everyone down there wanted us. It was like that every minute. Every morning we'd get to town, and then every evening we'd be running through their girls. Georgia, South Carolina, North Carolina, there was something in the water down there back in the 1980s. Because those girls were crazy, crazy, crazy. I'm surprised whenever we go back that we aren't greeted by hundreds of kids who look like us.

But I knew deep down that having indiscriminate sex was not a good thing. I just didn't have the character to say "no more."

It gets to the point where your attitude hardens, and you start to believe that that's what women are there for. They become objects.

I justified it to myself for a time by thinking that these are people who aren't necessarily going wild just because I'm a celebrity. Yes, they're fans of your music and they think you're cute and get some special thrill out of bedding a star, but they're doing the same thing with the grocery store clerk or the high-school basketball star or the doctor's son. They're not just living for the tour coming to L.A. so they can sleep with the Smokey Robinsons of the world. They're sleeping with the Smokey Robinsons within their own little world already.

A lot of times if you're onstage, you'll see someone and you'll send your security to get her and bring her back for you. But most of the time, they were back there already.

A lot of the promoters brought people around. That attitude of "I want to make sure y'all have a good time." Or, "Go to the after party. I'll have the girls there."

These aren't necessarily hookers, but they're known to the local promoters as party girls, women who will come on out and get wild if you put them in the right situation.

It's like if I'm doing a party and I'm hiring this band to come in, I'm going to have a band that's appropriate to the mood, one that will entertain everyone. That's the role of these women. They're as much a part of the party as ordering the food, drink, and music.

I never met anyone on the road that I wanted to spend more than one night with.

You're not going to see them again. It became a thing where I knew what this scene was all about. Oh, one-night stands. This is normal, this happens. They know it too. They aren't going to see me in the park tomorrow playing ball where they could come nag me.

It's not like what you would imagine groupies to be. Yes, the stakes are higher and the rewards are higher. But it's already going on in the rest of the world. There's just no barriers in my world of entertainment like there is in normal society.

That can cause all sorts of problems when something goes down.

Magic Johnson, for instance.

When the whole HIV-AIDS thing became the talk of the town, even before Magic Johnson, it slowed me down. But then you're already caught up because of that incubation period. You think, "Dag, that one night I did five years ago and they're saying it can stay in your system for ten years."

When Magic announced his problem, everybody ran around in a panic. I had a friend in L.A. who said when Magic Johnson came out and said that, all of L.A. was scared because all of L.A. was sleeping with everybody. So I know that a lot of people who were on the road when Magic made his announcement were scared to death.

Not that it stopped anybody for long. It took my marriage to get me out of that pattern.

I think one of the reasons I didn't indulge when we first went on the road is my upbringing. Again, I'm not saying that I was an angel—far from it—but I think the core values my parents gave me prevented me from ever getting into any serious trouble.

My parents have been married for over thirty-five years, and they're still together as I write this book. They are middle-class people from Hollis, Queens. Solid citizens.

Love and Marriage, Food and Family

We had a normal family life. My parents were always together, always steadily employed.

At home, my mother always cooked. She cooked for me like six people were coming over. Even when I was living there, she would cook.

Oh, and *can* she cook.

Chicken and collard greens. Macaroni and cheese—she makes the best macaroni and cheese and stuff. She goes all out every holiday.

I'm not really a spicy-foods person.

It's simple American food. Basically, always a three- or four-course meal. Oatmeal or cream of farina, Cream of Wheat. Bacon. Eggs. Toast. You know, tea. I used to love tea with milk in it, to make it turn light. You got to make it real sweet. I used to love that.

We always had liver and rice and peas or liver and rice and corn or fried chicken.

On Fourth of July, it was ribs and chicken. When I was a kid, you couldn't give me sweets, cake or nothing. I ate food.

My mother told me when I was around one years old, I used to walk around shouting, "Chicken. Chicken. Give me chicken." All my aunts thought it was so cute.

It was always the basic things. You know what I'm saying? That's why on that "Christmas in Hollis" record, I said, "It's Christmastime in Hollis, Queens. Mom's cooking / all chicken and collard greens / rice and stuff and macaroni and cheese. . . ." And it was always there. I knew what day of the week it was by what food we were having.

It was good, though. I used to love liver with the brown gravy over the rice, with either corn or green peas. And you mix the corn up into the gravy . . . that used to be good.

Even when my mother went away or she went to work, she precooked everything.

"This is in here, and put this in the oven." Breakfast, lunch, and dinner were always there. Four-course meals, every day of my life. My friends used to enjoy coming over to my house.

101

When I visit her now—you know, I don't want to hurt her feelings, but I'm tired of eating. She thinks I'm so skinny now. And she's still trying to get me to fatten up. It's like a nightmare.

I wasn't real adventurous in my eating habits. I didn't start eating Chinese food a lot until we moved from Hollis in 1987 to Freeport, Long Island. That's when I went to Chinese food. I guess I was bored. I went to every Chinese food place within a hundred block radius. Trying to find a spot I loved.

My typical early Run-DMC meal, though, like from when I first started to when I got diet-conscious, was three cheeseburgers—maybe sometimes three double cheeseburgers—large fries, and onion rings. That's what I would eat every day.

It had to be from Burger King.

Hated McDonald's. Wendy's was—you know, it was all right. Wendy's kind of tasted like home, but Burger King always grilled it. Even though they precooked the burger when they sent it down the little rack thing, flame was right there on it.

That diet almost caused the group to break up. I used to pass gas. The onion rings made me pass gas. They used to hate me to the point where they would starting yelling, "It ain't funny no more!"

My parents went through some crazy times when I finally left the house. Like many married couples, after they no longer had the children to focus on, it was like, "Who's this person here?"

I found out about that from my brother. It got to the point where they was going over my brother's house at like three or four in the morning. My father was calling my mom crazy and this and that, and said that my mother pulled a knife on him, and all types of wild stuff that I couldn't imagine from my parents when I was growing up.

As strange as that sounds, it was kind of a fight based on love. At the point they got into those wild fights, my father was retired and had diabetes. My mother kept insisting, "He's sick and he's lying about it. He's sick and he ain't telling nobody."

So finally I had to get over there and put everybody in order.

"Before you go to counseling, Dad, are you sick?"

"No, I'm not sick. I have diabetes and that's it."

"Would you tell us if you were going to die?"

So it went, my mom listening to it all.

"Yeah," my father insisted. "I'm telling you."

To this day she believes he's lying. But he says the only reason she's acting like this is because I left. There was no one left to worry about, and my mother is really overprotective.

Thankfully, they adjusted, and found out who that person across the dinner table was. Now they go out to dinner and do other things together. And, yes, they still argue.

The one area where my parents might have failed me is that they were being parents and not growing up with me. I was the type of son they wanted on the face—I was always a straight-A student, always on time, a do-gooder, for the most part.

But at the same time, I was smoking and drinking and illin'. You know what I'm saying? I'm smoking angel dust and doing all the wild stuff my parents think I ain't doing because of what I'm presenting to them.

I never asked my father if he smoked reefer. But I know he smoked cigarettes, although never in the house. And he never used to smoke around me, but I remember being little and strapped in the front seat and he had cigarettes in the glove compartment of the car. I used to take them out and look at them.

My parents were always hardworking, on time, on point, never failed, taking care of business. And, you know, that was instilled in me. So that I was always on time, on point, taking care of business, even when I would come crashing home after drinking.

My brother, Alford, is three years older than I am. We're not really close, but we get along okay.

Alford is basically a Star Trek and science fiction fiend. Comic book collector. That part of him was a big inspiration to me. I used to take the comic books and I used to draw Spider-Man and all of them. But basically, Alford was like really, really quiet.

He worked for Con Edison for the last seven years, the guy who goes down in the hole. All my homeboys are always telling me, "Yeah. I seen your brother coming out the hole." Or "I was driving and I seen Alford all over Queens."

Alford's personality would make a good sitcom. He's the hardworking guy that mumbles and complains and don't like nobody or nothing. You know what I'm saying? He's a nice guy. But he's like Archie Bunker and George Jefferson rolled up into one. Just a hardworking, can't beat-the-system guy.

Even when we were growing up he was like that, to a degree.

He knew what friends of mine that he didn't like and he knew why he didn't like them. He had good reasons not to like them. And he told me, point-blank.

"He's lunch meat" and "He's this and that" and "He's this lowlife." And it was true. And even when he told me I knew it was true, but I was, "Oh, I'm just trying to be cool," or whatever.

You know, he's the guy that first bought the turntables and the mixer. He used to do smart things with his money, and he had his hobbies.

He DJ'd. He knew how to spin back and DJ. He wasn't into the rap aspect of it. We used to go down into the basement and duel, just me and him.

He was really good. I mean, really good.

The difference is, Alford stayed down in the basement making his own tapes.

He had enough skills to walk on up to the park. "Yo. I'm a DJ. Can I get on?"

But he was never into that. It was just another thing for him to do when he wasn't watching Star Trek and reading his comic books. That was more important to him.

I don't think he was ever jealous of my success. It was just DJing and rapping to him, something he'd been watching me do in the basement for years. He never wanted it for himself. He'd comment occasionally on our beats, or give a little criticism. But he lived his life and did what he wanted to do.

I don't speak to him that often. My mother always tells me, "Call your brother." My wife always tries to make me call him. And his wife tries to make him call me.

But it's like, we know. You know what I'm saying? Because even when we're together, we don't make excuses. We just look at each other.

We might go out to dinner occasionally. Or we'll get together on Thanksgiving and my mother will say, "Y'all need to hang to-gether."

But when I see him, he's Alford, I'm Darryl. That's it. We don't need to see each other often to know that.

My marriage isn't at all like my parents'. It's completely different.

We have a vast age difference, for one. My mom and dad are within a couple of years of each other. My wife is ten years younger than me.

Another difference is our attitude toward home life. My parents are from a generation that saved as a matter of course. My wife and I have long-term goals, but they aren't quite what my parents' were. We're saving for my son's college education and all that, but it's almost like we're living day-by-day instead of looking at one future goal, which I think my parents always did.

You know, we have our crazy arguments. And that's when we are dealing with marriage.

But for the most part, we deal with each other in a lot of the same ways we did when we were boyfriend/girlfriend. That's when I feel the love is coming like when we first met. When you aren't arguing and dealing with anything serious, the interaction is boy-friend/girlfriend puppy love.

I think with my parents it was always hard work and business. It was just different trying to raise the kids. They bought a house. As soon as I was born, my father and mother bought a house.

They were very proud of that. My mother would always say, "I had a house when I was twenty-three years old. We worked for our house."

My wife comes from a household where she and her sister were raised by their father, so she has a different experience. But she also had stability growing up, so she knows what it is to have a loving home.

When she's kidding me, she tells me that living with me reminds her of home. Her joke is that her father and I get along so well because we're the same age (he's a good ten years older, for the record).

There is no true ideal age to get married.

But if you press me, I would say twenty-five is a good age to pick. Because I think anything under that is, well, still too young.

To me, it doesn't sound right when you see a young couple and they're twenty-three years old. A lot happens in those two years.

At least by twenty-five, you either did everything that you needed to do or you knew about those things but didn't want to do them, so now you know you don't have to worry about what you didn't do or your need to still do it. I think at twenty-five, you're able to say, "All right. I'm twenty-five and once I'm into this marriage, it's on. I gotta handle my responsibilities."

That's been a sore point in my marriage. My wife is a lot younger and really didn't do a lot of the things that I did. Her beef is, "Why did God give you the right to go out and have all that fun with your career, going around the world, and I can't do that?"

So it's difficult. Jay has had the same problem. His wife is, I think, six years younger than him. When he first met her, she was seventeen. So they went through their relationship, and then about three or four years down the road, I met my wife.

Jay was ready with advice. "Yo, D. You gonna have problems.

You definitely going to have a problem because your wife's younger than you. So you gotta be ready for that."

Women have always been around Run-DMC. Even when we first started, the other guys in the group were involved with someone. Run was already married and living with his wife and kids. Jay had a girl that he lived with. They always would tell about the domestic headaches. I was the single guy, living at home with my folks, not a care in the world.

We'd be leaving at six in the morning to go to a show and him and Joe were in the bus moping about their wive—we'd call them wives, even if they weren't married, because they'd been together forever—driving them crazy.

Then they'd look at me. "Don't never get married."

I lived with my parents until I got married. So I always had more money than the other guys. I was available to drop everything and be anywhere at a moment's notice.

This worked out fine in the days when I was the single guy in the band. But when I first started bringing my wife around, a funny thing happened. It was almost like my wife took me away from another woman. In this case, that other woman was my group.

Run couldn't call me every two minutes and say, "Hey, D. Be here." Or ask me over and over, "You going to be there? You gotta be there, man. You know, you gonna mess everything up for me." The dynamic of Run-DMC really changed.

We still tried to operate. But it was like a big thing that D got a girl now.

I remember seeing my wife for the first time.

When I saw her, I knew. If she's not married, that's my wife, I told myself. That's all I can say. It might not work, God, I don't know. But if she's not married, that's the look, that's the attitude—that's gotta be it. If you see a picture of D with his wife, that's it.

I was always shy. Always. But I somehow found the nerve to approach my wife.

We were going to go over to Russell Simmons's house to negotiate the *Down with the King* album. Run was late, so me and Jay went to get some carrot juice. That's when I was on my health kick.

We were walking down Broadway when I saw her. She was with her friend.

Of course, it was her friend who noticed me. "Oh, you know who that is? That's Run! That's Run!"

Well, we were off to a flying start. But I knew from the minute I saw her.

Zuri was a little shy. She told us she lived in Hartford, Connecticut, and she thought Run-DMC was a white group.

Okay. So much for my celebrity status.

She said she knew LL. They loved LL, New Edition, and groups like that, but she wasn't into Run-DMC. That actually made me feel better. Okay. At least I'm not dealing with groupies.

So her friend asked for an autograph, and we signed. As I looked at her, I had to know. "Are you married?" She looked older. And actually, she carried herself as if she was older than she was. And then I asked her for her phone number.

I knew it right then.

So began our puppy-love stage. Our first date was five days later. I thought a lot about where to go. I finally took her to City Island in the Bronx for seafood and clams. Even though City Island is where everybody takes their girls, it's nice.

And so we decided, after a short courtship, to get married.

She was eighteen and I was twenty-eight.

She had done a few things. She had appeared as a dancer on *Club MTV.* But at age eighteen, you're just starting out. I was twenty-eight, already had been on a world tour.

But when you get married, you know, everything changes. They say marriage is the wake-up call. Sometimes it's hard to hear that alarm clock.

So I try to compromise.

People applaud us because we've been married for seven years. Seven years! My parents have been married for over thirty-five years. Quite a change in attitude from those days.

I really think it's possible for someone to be married forever. But marriage is not the same as the love thing. Marriage is really an agreement to stay together. Because no one goes around loving each other twenty-four hours a day.

I mean, me and Zuri went through some really shaky times, divorce-talking times. You know what I'm saying?

But it's good to say that word and let it out.

Most marriages aren't tested by sickness and death, contrary to what your vows are all about. No, the key question is whether two different spirits can get along.

If you're able to argue and then say, "I don't agree with what you're saying, but tomorrow's another day," that's what marriage is. That's what the "for better or for worse part" is. Because every day you'll be confronted with a difference of opinion. It's within that compromise that love exists.

It was when my wife and I had our crazy arguments that I truly saw that my wife and I were married. That's when we were dealing with *Marriage,* capital M, and not just any other relationship.

Where do most of the conflicts come in?

Mostly from me not wanting to do all the things that she wants to do. Because I've been there and did that and I'm older now and that doesn't excite me no more.

I just was with people for the last three weeks and you want me to come home and still be social? I want to come home and hide in my house and just sit and chill. Or else do Dad sort of stuff, like take my son to Chuck E. Cheese's.

But I can't blame her. She's tied up with our son most of the time.

So, if you're in a relationship that you want to maintain for a long time, here's my advice: you have to respect this person you're with before you love them. Before the love, before the fun, before the kids, you got to respect your spouse as the person that he or she is, and the person he or she is becoming.

People change. That's a given. I am not the same person I was before I got married. A lot of the conflicts we've had come from that.

When we first started dating, we did amusement parks and all of that, but once we got into this "marriage" mode, it became more like a business agreement.

In order to make this business work, this business of husband/wife, mother/father to this kid, to do what we got to do, you have to respect me regardless of what I do or what I don't do.

You might not like it, you might hate it, you might want to change me tomorrow, but if I am not going to change, that's something you are going to have to grant me, if that's the decision I am going to make.

And I've never told my wife this, but if you don't like that, then there's one solution. I will leave or you will leave.

Unless you respect the person and let them be that person that they are, it's not going to work.

Now, I can almost hear what you're saying to yourself. I'm intolerant. Far from it. I don't think that either person should change anything about them. Then you can really see if this is meant to be.

I tell my wife, "Be who you are. I don't want you to change a thing." I respect you for whatever you want to do. I don't put any boundaries on her. She can go out with her friends and all that. A lot of her male friends are amazed by that.

But that's something that she needs to do. I might not want to go to the movies and laugh and giggle, but you can go out. You can go out to parties. She goes to parties and football players come up to her and say, "You're married? How old are you? You are a baby! You mean to tell me DMC is letting you go out?!"

But I respect her enough to know that she is not going to

fool around on me. I know that if I leave her in the house, it's going to destroy her.

You are who you are. I am who I am. Let's make this thing work.

Bad Habits

I was probably age eleven when I had my first drink and smoked my first reefer.

Why did we do it? Because the older guys were. But we couldn't hang with them and we didn't have as much money as they had, so we had to go get us something to do. And I guess that's how I began to experiment with controlled substances.

When we were around age ten, me and Nathan and Jocko from my block used to go and collect cigarette butts off the ground. We'd get a whole bunch of them and then sit there and smoke them, passing them around. We didn't know where they'd been. I mean, just butts off the ground, and we'd be putting them up to our lips and puffing away.

When we graduated to reefer, I have to think that the signs were there when I'd come back into my house. My parents aren't dumb. They probably know I was doing drugs, maybe, maybe not. I used to come home and go in my room, and my eyes would sometimes be red, and I'd have about ten of the classic symptoms of drug use.

Even if they knew I was smoking reefer, I'm sure they never dreamed about some of the harder drugs I did. The things I'm about to tell you about are going to bug my mom out. She was always overprotective. I can hear her now: "Cocaine?! What!!"

In the early days, Larry Smith used to always drive us to shows in his big long Sedan DeVille Caddy; Larry Smith, me, Jay, Run—that was like *the core*. It was only us traveling in the beginning. But that was enough to have a party every night.

Every club in the tristate area, every show, from Connecticut to Boston to the Bronx, there was nothing but drugs everywhere. Everywhere we'd visit.

I remember one show where it was really out of control. It was Run-DMC, Treacherous Three, Fearless Four, the Furious Five with Melle Mel making a guest appearance. Mr. Magic was hosting it. I mean, just about everybody was doing cocaine; the girls, the radio people, the promoters. Everybody knew where to get it. Every tour that we did in the early days—the Fresh Fest, the *Raising Hell* tour, even with the Beastie Boys, people were getting high all around me.

I mean, not partying type of high. High as a way of life, twenty-four/seven high.

Every tour in the early days, every tour that I did in the eighties, people did drugs, got drunk, or got high in some form or another. The Beasties, they said they was into taking mushrooms.

When we went to Amsterdam—oh my God, everybody was living in the Bulldog, a reefer bar. They would sit in there day after day and smoke reefer and eat the reefer cakes and cookies. It was like those myths about the lotus-eaters. We had to drag people out of there, they were staying so long.

But understand—it was so widespread, everybody was doing it. We'd go to a photo shoot and the photographer was getting high.

I think ultimately that's why I abused drugs. I had money, I had more money than most everybody around. I went from a dime of coke to an eighth in no time. I could say when I toured with Whodini, when I toured with LL, when I toured with the Beasties, almost everybody was getting high, doing drugs in some form or another.

Cocaine, reefer, beer, liquor, and mushrooms. The funny thing is, because we weren't sticking needles into our arms, we assured ourselves we weren't drug addicts.

There are some exceptions. I have never seen Will Smith smoke reefer or do cocaine, but I can imagine he probably drank a beer and got high one night. But that's about it. He was as straight as they come, as amazing as that may seem about someone who's a worldwide superstar.

I've been through an encyclopedia of drug use in my day.

And the one question everyone always asks is—did you do heroin?

No. It was never really around us. I knew there were people in Hollis that did, sniffing mostly, not shooting. We called it P-Dope.

I did some LSD blotter paper one time before we did a show at Roseland in New York. A Puerto Rican girl gave it to me and my friend T. It was a little paper you put on your tongue, a tab of acid. I took that and was up all night until like 1:00 P.M. the next day.

I was so high that me and T took the train home, even though I had driven my car to the club. I had to go back and get it. I don't know what I was doing.

I also used to smoke angel dust a lot. Getting dusted is like somebody taking a vice grip and tightening it, but without pain. You know how your hand or foot goes to sleep when you're sitting in one position for a long time? That's what smoking angel dust is like. Imagine walking like you're in a dream, taking really high steps.

Run said I used to bug out. "D, you were smoking dust like every day for three weeks straight." Mostly because it came to Hollis and everybody had it.

I didn't feel like I was losing myself to it. It was just something to do when you're bored to death.

There's a price to pay for living on the edge.

If you try to live up to your own hype—"I'm hard, rough, tough, I am a player, ghetto killer, gangbanger"—it causes things to happen around you, even if you don't want them to be set off. Case in point: Puffy Combs and his shooting incident in the New York nightclub.

Here he is, out having a drink, and someone had to throw some dollars in his face because he's all about the Benjamins. Next thing you know, someone pulls out a gun, he's hopping in a getaway car, and the police are arresting him and Jennifer Lopez.

Once again, though, I have to confess that I fell victim to this same attitude, carrying my career into my lifestyle, and vice versa. I've made that mistake. Believe me, I've made it.

Around the end of 1990, going into 1991, I started saying, "Hey, me drinking this Olde English malt liquor onstage is really sending a bad message." I mean, I was going beyond getting buzzed. Like my first ventures in performing, I was drinking to the point where I would be stinking drunk onstage.

This bodyguard friend of mine took some pictures of our tours. One shot is of the cases of Olde English we shipped over to Europe because they didn't have any on sale (ironically, not even in England). My wife couldn't believe it when she saw the photos, and started laughing, "You mean to tell me you shipped Olde English over there?"

Yes, we did. It was as necessary as a toothbrush in those days.

But that sort of behavior was starting to wear on me, mentally at first, later physically. Here I am, sending out a message to so many people, and they're responding with love and the desire to be like me, yet I can't tell them to take better care of themselves?

I mean, people started wearing Adidas because of us, people started dressing like us, and people wanted to wear the Cazals like me. And while that was fine, I had to wonder what I was doing to them by staggering around onstage.

My partner Run and I are like, "Dag, I'm telling people by my behavior that it's okay to get pissy drunk, no matter what the circumstances." It's like I'm saying I don't give a damn.

And if I don't, why should you?

I felt badly about it, because we were constantly trying to hold ourselves up as role models. We were constantly doing lectures at schools and talking to kids. Parents were always telling us how much the kids loved my group.

Gangsta rap was happening right at the beginning of the 1990s. We were one of the few old-school groups that was still out there when it blew up big, when the FBI and local law enforcement groups and Time Warner started attacking Ice-T and N.W.A. And the same people who were telling us how much their kids loved us started asking us why the other groups can't be like Run-DMC.

If they only knew the truth, they wouldn't have bothered. If they would have patted me down, they'd have found out that I'm sitting with cocaine in my pockets.

I've thought a lot about the way drinking and drugs are used in our society. After all, they've been with us since biblical times, and probably will be forever in one form or another. And yes, there's a difference between use and abuse.

I was using drugs and alcohol for both good and bad reasons at one point.

According to the Bible, you might drink some wine just to make merry for a minute. And early on it also had some medicinal uses, like all alcohol in the days before anesthetics were widespread.

But in modern times, we use it for more than physical pain. It blocks out those feelings that we'd rather not deal with. That was my problem.

There's an old saying: Where there's no discipline, abuse runs wild. I'm not sure if I buy that, but certainly I feel that it takes discipline in order to drink. If you can discipline yourself—the scenario of, "We are having a little dinner, invite over some good friends I haven't seen in a long time, and let's drink a little wine so we can bring up all those memories"—then alcohol is society's friend. But it's when you get beyond that that it gets scary.

I remember Dr. Timothy Leary, the noted professor and LSD experimental guru of the 1960s, once said that if you take LSD, you'll be closer to God. In books I've read on ancient mysticism, there are writings that also say people drink to get closer to God.

Maybe people take hard drugs and abuse alcohol to visit other planes and dimensions and levels that do exist but that would take deep meditation or even death to reach. We, as humans, want fast everything. Quick divorces, microwavable food—it's easy to see the way our society is.

Not surprising that people abuse drugs and alcohol to get to that level, instead of trying to get there spiritually.

It sometimes may seem that celebrities are more prone to abuse of drugs and alcohol than so-called regular people. They really aren't. Before you're a celebrity, you're on the same level as everybody else. Me and Run were just like everybody else. We wanted to get high, beginning at an early age.

Why did I get high when I was younger? The first reason was I thought I had to do it to be cool. People I looked up to did it.

Bad Habits

Like the older teenagers. The teenagers with girlfriends. They had cigarettes and they had the Adidas on, they had everything I wanted.

I thought in order to be down with the older guys, the tough guys, the hard rocks, the B-boys in the neighborhood, you got to smoke cigarettes, drink beer, and smoke reefer.

When you become a celebrity, the same feelings exist. Only now you can afford to do it. Where you used to have to find two other people so you all could put in a dollar each to get a three-dollar bag of reefer, you can go out and buy an ounce and have all the reefer and weed you want.

So for whatever reason you're getting high in life, when you become a celebrity, you just get more of it, based on the same desire, the same drive, the same intention of getting high in the first place. You can satisfy it triplefold.

But let me say this: it isn't even a matter of being a celebrity sometimes. When we first had our record "It's Like That" / "Sucker M.C.'s," we were already out of control. We were all getting so high, sniffing coke and drinking and partying so much and so often, it became a normal way of life. None of us thought we were drug addicts.

We were wrong about that.

Yeah, it was all one big party back in the day. But I'll never forget the moment I realized I had to do something about my weight.

It was in 1988 and we were on tour. We had some time to kill in Los Angeles, so we were walking around the Fox Hills Mall. It's something you do on the road because, aside from the shows, a lot of touring is killing time.

I was hungry this day. And I wanted to get my favorite, fried chicken. So we were on chicken patrol as we were walking in the mall, and this guy just walked up to me and asked us for an autograph.

As we signed his scrap of paper, the guy looked me and said,

"Living gooood." And he patted me on my stomach. I had a pot-belly there.

It's hard to describe that feeling. The power of the relationship between fan and musician shifted 180 degrees at that moment.

I remember that day soooo much, so vividly. For the next few days—hell, the next few months and years, and likely for the rest of my life—I kept hearing him saying that.

"Living gooood."

I owe that guy, in a strange way, although I wish he had delivered the message in a more subtle manner. That was the moment when I said, "I ain't going to eat the Burger King stuff no more. I'm going to eat regular food now."

So I started eating sensibly. And sensibly, as I learned, doesn't necessarily mean that I cut out the Burger King stuff.

I'd still go get a Whopper. But I cut down on the number of them I'd eat. I'd just get a Whopper and fries and a soda. That's one meal instead of three. I knew instinctively that you had to eat in order to really lose weight the way you want to, 'cause if you don't eat, your body is going to starve and go after the muscle cells first.

Losing weight became my obsession. I started reading everything I could on the topic, basically watching how much I ate.

I also began exercising. This was also a self-starting thing. I would watch ESPN workout shows and read all the health and nutrition magazines in airports when we were waiting for a flight. When I got home from the road, I bought a bench and weights and put them in my house.

I picked it up on my own. I had a personal trainer for maybe three weeks, because I was getting bored with doing it. But then I got tired of having him, so now I'm back to doing it myself.

I do forty-five minutes to an hour of cardio, which is either riding a bike or walking on a StairMaster or a treadmill, all while listening to music. I cannot do it without my music.

At one time I was doing weights every day, and you're not supposed to do that. That just defeats the purpose. Then I was doing weights every other day. But now I do them every two to three days. Full body workout, chest, back, arms, shoulders, legs, calves, and sit-ups.

Just enough to keep myself lean. I don't want to get big, because when you do that, it looks bulky. It's part of my life now. I can't live without it, and it drives my wife crazy. She says I'm obsessed with it.

While I was busy reshaping my body and my eating habits, I still had one bad vice. That would come back to haunt me.

While I finally got around to paying attention to the food I put into my body, I was still drinking those Olde English forty-ounce malt liquors as my main beverage. It got to the point where I had cut so far back on food that it seemed like I wasn't eating at all.

Drinking on an empty stomach practically ruined my insides.

When I was eating the three cheeseburgers, I used to down the forties and it didn't have any effect. I guess all that food had something to do with that.

Of course, I started wasting away. And the rumor mill got out of control for a while. People were saying, "D, you losing a lot of weight." Crack was real popular around that time, so a lot of people felt I was doing that.

The chaotic schedule of life on the road and my desire to cut back on food created some weird patterns for me.

If I was real drunk on a particular day, I would eat only once that day, and then not much at that meal. Other days, I'd head out to Red Lobster and gorge.

Today, I can't stand lobster because I used to eat it so often. I'd arrive at Red Lobster, order fried shrimp, two rock lobster tails, shrimp cocktail, appetizers, bread, and that would be my meal. Because I had money, I was living the good life. You're *eatin'*.

Of course, this caught up with me. Did it ever.

I woke up one morning and had a sharp pain in my side. I figured that it was the way I slept that morning, maybe something I twisted from sleeping in an awkward position or making a strange move onstage. You're leaping around up there, paying attention to the crowd and the whole atmosphere, a little pissy from the forties, and you can get injured pretty easily. It usually doesn't show up until you calm down a few hours later.

But this pain didn't seem to go away. There was a period of about six months where it would come and go away, come and go away. We were on the road at the time in support of our *Back from Hell* album, so I really didn't have time to get it checked out.

It didn't really bother me when I was onstage. It only happened about three or four times when I was performing. I thought it was because I ate too much, or didn't eat enough. Then I had started drinking a lot of rum-and-Cokes, and figured maybe the soda was causing it. Yeah, that's it. Drinking and eating. Indigestion. Heartburn. That kind of thing.

Then it started coming more frequently. I still wasn't worried that it was serious, but started thinking that maybe I should slow down a bit, or at least watch what I ate.

Finally we got off the road, and I thought I'd have time to rest and finally get better. It wasn't to be.

I woke up one morning and the pain was worse than ever. It was like someone was stabbing me in my stomach over and over and over. I was in crazy agony. It was the craziest thing that ever happened to me.

Every time I'd felt this pain before though, it would eventually go away. So I got up, got dressed, took a shower, went outside, did my normal routine, hoping against hope that this was just a flare-up. I even went out and got a beer that morning, thinking it might take some hair of the dog to calm me down.

It was toward the afternoon and I was hanging out with this guy who worked for us, Garfield. I told him I was going to go home because I wasn't feeling well. I thought if I went home and laid down and didn't drink or eat too much, I'd bounce back.

Well, I get home and thought better of that plan. Maybe I better eat something, since all I've had today was beer. Maybe it's just that my stomach's empty (I tried every rationalization there was, believe me).

So I had a steak with some rice and vegetables, a nice balanced meal.

But then it got worse.

My mother came home about four in the afternoon from her job as a nurse. I met her at the door. "Mom, don't come in. Turn around. I gotta go to the hospital." And she just looked at me and didn't even ask any questions. Usually she asks what's wrong. But she looked at me and I couldn't stand up straight. I had to stay bent over.

I had never said anything to her about the pains. My mom is a worrier, and I didn't want to add to her burdens, particularly since it was something I thought was nothing serious.

We get to the emergency room and bureaucracy takes over. I'm in crazy pain, bent over, and they made me sit down and fill out the forms. Here I am, it's like someone is stabbing me in the gut, and I'm doing paperwork.

Filling out the sheet took twenty to twenty-five minutes of agony. While we were sitting, I was like, "Ma. They gotta take me now. They gotta take me now." And she would go up to the front and they would say, "Wait a minute. You'll get your chance. It's gotta go in order of seriousness."

I was like, "Ain't nobody in here shot in the head! I'm really in pain!"

Finally my turn comes. They take me back into this area where the rooms are created by curtains separating various beds. I get in there and it's another fifteen minutes of waiting in agonizing pain.

When a doctor came in, he first thought I had a problem with my appendix.

"Lay back."

No, I can't lay back. And don't touch me. All they had to do was touch me and it was like I was going to pass out.

So he looked at me and asked, "Do you drink?"

And I was like, "Yeah. I drink beer, malt liquor."

"Well, how many cans do you drink a day?"

I was like, "Twelve."

He was like, "Twelve cans a day?"

I was like, "No. Twelve forty-ounce bottles."

Once I said that he looked at me like, "What?!!!" I remember his eyes widened.

Right then, he knew he was going to sign me in. "He's not going home. Put him with an intravenous and we'll run some tests on him."

So there I am in the hospital. They couldn't give me anything for this crazy pain I was in because they didn't know what was wrong. But they did remember to come and take blood from me what seemed like every hour. My arms were sore by the time I got out of the hospital, I was so drained by the needles.

By 11:00 A.M. the next morning, they knew what it was. Pancreatitis. An inflamed pancreas.

Now, if you're like me, you don't know much about the pancreas. It's an oblong-shaped, flat gland that is an integral part of your digestive system, sandwiched between the stomach and the spine, quietly doing its job of secreting digestive enzymes and insulin. They help break down the food as it travels through your body's intestinal system.

You'd never really care you had one until it suddenly starts barking. Then it becomes one of the most important organs in your body.

The doctor told me, "Thank God it wasn't your liver. This is treatable."

"Fine," I said. "How will you treat it? What will you give me?"

"Nothing," he said. They can't give you medicine, because you can't take anything into your body while your pancreas is inflamed. They have to wait until all the acid in the bile ducts drains off and reduces the inflammation. So they gave me intravenous vitamins, but that's it.

You can't die from pancreatitis, but there were times I wished I could have. I was in the hospital for three weeks, all of it in agony. I mean, it hurt to breathe. After a while, you just drift into this netherworld of trying to do anything to take your mind off it.

After about a week, they started giving me some drugs to ease me up, but it was always there, a constant presence. I was in another world. I just laid in bed all the time. For some reason, I remember watching *Leave It to Beaver* at 4:00 A.M. in the morning every night, finally drifting off to sleep shortly after it was over.

From touring the world to laying there watching TV.

It was three weeks before I could breathe normally without pain.

Strangely enough, there were times when I was laying in the hospital thinking, "Oh, this is just what I need." I was taken out of the Burger King/drinking loop and given some real nutrition.

They was giving me clear liquids, jello, soup broth, grilled chicken breast with rice, stuff like that. They wanted to slowly reintroduce my system to eating food. Nothing fried, nothing oily.

Finally, near the end of my hospital stay, my doctor came back to visit. The news he had wasn't good.

You could go through this again if you drink, he told me. It could come back tomorrow. That's the seriousness of it. I had to learn to love my pancreas. It was like I could either drink and die, or never drink again and never inflame it again.

After going through three weeks of pain like that, it was an easy choice. It was something I had to live with.

Still, the temptation was there. I had to test it. After I got out of the hospital, we went to Germany on tour and Run said, "Here, D. Take a sip of this wine. It ain't gonna hurt you."

At the time my system was kind of purging itself of years of abuse. I was going to the bathroom a lot and—excuse me for being frank—I had diarrhea all the time.

So when I took a sip of the wine, it was like a bomb went off in my system. We were parked on the tour bus, and I had to sprint off and run to a nearby Burger King. That's how volatile it was.

Since drinking that wine, I haven't touched a drop. Those days of twelve forty-ounce bottles are a distant memory. And the rest of my system is skittish as well. I'm really restricted in what I can eat, so I get a funny feeling in my stomach if I eat some fish and it's been bathed in wine and butter sauce. I get a tingling in my stomach. I know when there's alcohol in something.

I have an eating plan now, versus just eating for the sake of eating. I admit it's not for everyone. But it works for me.

When I go to Burger King, I might order a lot of hamburgers. But I don't eat the bread, I'll just eat the meat. The protein diet, and I thought of it before it became popular.

My family rarely eats dinner together. Once in a while, my wife will cook, but I'll opt for either Apple Jacks or corn flakes. But I'll sit there at the table with my son and we'll have family time.

Zuri will try to keep my son from eating just cereal, like Daddy eats. She wants me to give him Cream of Wheat.

I'm not claiming I'm perfect in what I eat now. I still can eat a whole box of SnackWell's cookies, or a lot of Rice Krispies treats. So I'll get eight of those and eat a whole box of SnackWell's cookies knowing damn sure that I'm hungry for dinner, and then I'll go and eat dinner. And then I'll be hurt and I'll be sitting there, "I'm hurt, honey."

And I do that a lot. And that's not good, you know what I'm saying? It's not good.

Run-DMC has adjusted our collective behavior a bit as we've gotten older.

On our contract riders, we ask for deli platters, preferably with turkey breast. Inevitably, even though we say we don't want any red meat, they'll mix it with roast beef.

We ask for fish, chicken, but not Kentucky Fried. And if it's got to be Kentucky Fried, it's got to be extra-crispy, because their original recipe is the worst. We also request a fruit platter, cranberry juice, and Hennessey, for the crew. That's standard, and then we ask for hot meals for ourselves as well.

The other guys nibble. Sometimes we don't even eat it because it'll be wrong. I don't ever eat it. I can't eat when I go onstage. I don't like feeling full when I'm up there.

That's now. I used to glutton out when we were on the *Raising Hell* tour and we had catering. I used to sit there and pig out before hitting the stage. Truly "raising hell."

All that's changed since I stopped drinking. Of all the changes I've made in my life, that's been the biggest.

Now, the big question: do I miss it?

I don't miss it. Because I'm mad I ever got high in the first place. I thought that I had to experience all of that in order to be able to say whether or not it was a bad thing to do.

I was totally wrong. I'm going to hit you right on the head with the reason. The reason why you don't have to is personified by Chuck D, the leader of Public Enemy.

I love Chuck D. Not because I consider him the prophet of the black youth and all of that stuff. And not because of his militant stance. It's just when I heard him, I thought he was God on the mike because of his voice and the way he put his lyrics together. To this day, when you ask me who was the best rapper I ever heard in my life, Chuck D wins the prize. You should hear how he kicks it to this day.

But I was crushed when Chuck D said he never smoked or drank anything. It was a blow to me, a realization that all my rationales for doing everything I had been doing were out the window. It's like the man who takes steroids in order to be the best bodybuilder, abuses his health, and then finds out another won the contest without using anything.

I was like, you mean this guy whose voice is so incredible, who makes the hardest music and beats, the biggest B-boy gangsta killer rapper—he never smoked reefer or nothing?! Where is all of this stuff out of his mouth coming from? He made me realize you can actually achieve this state of mind and being without getting high.

When he said that, I personally felt it took something away from me. And then I started bugging, felt ashamed, said I wished my mind was never touched and never altered.

But then I came to the realization that it is possible to exist in this world and still be cool, effective, to still be powerful, to still be self-confident and self-assured and not get high. And he's that example.

I've seen it in my own life. Now I don't get high and I feel I am writing better than I was back in the day. Now I'm just writing from the heart and it's coming out ten times better. Now I can feel what I want.

But this is after seven years. Looking back, the reefer made me think too much. I would just start thinking wild stuff, sad stuff. Alcohol made me fearless.

I now realize why I don't like saying anything, why I am not really talkative to people, the Quiet Storm. I have enough confidence to speak softly.

Now that I'm an old-timer, I don't smoke anymore.

I was just out on the Family Values tour with Limp Bizkit, Korn, and a lot of the younger alternative bands. The drug scene has definitely changed. People don't get high out in the open anymore, because it's not looked at as a normal thing to do. People don't think it's cool anymore. As far as the available women, that's still there. But drugs?

Harder to see, but it's still there.

And those that are not into the heavy drugs, they're definitely drinking a lot. I mean, drinking has almost overcome getting high. When you do drugs, you go in your closet and do it. But smoking reefer and drinking are still everywhere.

I was really worried the first time I ever went onstage sober. We used to drink heavily before, during, and after the shows.

It was a big journey for me. I remember asking myself, "Can I do this and not be drunk off of beer?" I thought I was going to feel different about performing, because the beer gave me a false sense of confidence.

That was instilled in me practically from day one of Run-DMC. Remember the show at the Roxy? It was held in front of the whole Zulu Nation, a big Bronx gang. A tough crowd, one that wasn't willing to take excuses.

Run and I argued backstage about who would go out to do the intro.

"You go out there."

"No, you go out there."

Finally Run pushed me out from behind the curtains, so I had to react. And that's when I thought of the entrance that we did on "Here We Go":

"1, 2, 3 / in the place to be / he is DJ Run / and I am DMC / funky fresh from 1983."

I felt that a little beer helped then. You know, made me quick with the wit.

More than anything, I wondered if the energy level was going to be there when we did the show sober. Could I be in a good mood without that boost?

I have to admit, the majority of our shows, particularly toward the end of my drinking days, I was drunk. I fell more than a few times, and the crew would just go, "D, you was pissy last night onstage."

But part of the whole thing was we smoked bags of reefer and drank Southern Comfort and then rhymed for hours. I didn't know if the stuff I wrote was because of the beer or in spite of it.

What I found out was that I can do it. Now that I'm not high onstage, I'm more comfortable with the parts where the other guy has his turn. Run can do a long speech, and I don't come out and ad-lib over it. I stand, patiently waiting for my turn.

I wonder what our career would have been like without the drinking and drugs. I know it would have been different.

In the beginning, the good times we had getting high off the stage were almost the only thing that held us together, same as it was the thing that held us together as friends when we were younger. And when we started getting money, we got more drugs and had more fun. Smoke reefer, rhyme. Smoke reefer, rhyme. Because we did that before we even made a record.

That's why things are changing now because we're all older and we got wives and kids.

I can only imagine the things I was doing when I was high onstage.

Run talks about the nights that he was always smokin' reefer, and he has his regrets as well. But the one night we always come back to is an incident that happened in Amsterdam.

C+C Music Factory happened to be there performing. Run was in the club, and he was admittedly drunk. At several points in the show, he ran up onstage and started dancing with them. You know? And everyone was looking at him. But he was having a good time. Didn't think about whether it went over well or not.

I've done that myself a couple of times, intruding on shows when I probably should have left well enough alone. I remember a show with Heavy D and somebody else where I went up onstage real drunk and sort of acted the fool. God, I can imagine how I looked.

Besides allowing me to clean up my insides, the stay in the hospital also allowed me to examine my life's path and answer the question What does it mean to be a man?

I always thought there was a certain point in life where your elders, your guardian, your father or mother will tell you, "Today's the day you became a man."

But now I realize that it's not a day that arrives, and no one will tell you when it happens. I think that what it means to be a man is to have a sense of responsibility. And I think it goes to the heart of it to say that you're here to create things, and whatever you create, you're responsible for that thing. Whether it's good or bad, whatever happens, I think the whole purpose of man is that he has the freedom to create—but that he has to answer for his creations.

And I think once you realize that, that's when the journey into manhood has begun.

My stay in the hospital is what made that crystal clear to me.

I was twenty-six years old when my hospitalization occurred. Having spent three weeks in agony, I had a lot of time to contemplate what had brought me to that point in life.

That's when I concluded that nobody was responsible for me being in there except me. And that realization made me realize I was a man now. I had to put away the childish behaviors I had indulged in for those many years.

From that point on, it was my responsibility to live life the right way.

I had very little discipline in my life before that. From age twelve, I was running around, drinking, doing drugs, hanging out, doing everything. I thought I was already a man because I had a driver's license, I was old enough to drink, I didn't have a curfew, I had a wonderful career that I thought I was in control of.

You know? The world was mine. I was the world's most eligible bachelor. No one had any dominion over me. I knew I was a man.

Three weeks of agony later, I knew I wasn't a man. The pain had grabbed me by the shirt and brought me to my senses. A man doesn't drink so much that he winds up in a hospital bed.

When I had recovered and came back to the world, my eyes had been opened. It was hard to go back to the same crew, the same lifestyle, and stay clean and sober. I never looked down on anybody, or took an attitude that I'm better than anybody who still indulges. But I started questioning people's actions in my own mind.

Like, "Dag, how can they do that?" He's still doing the same things we were doing since we were kids. It was like, "Damn, he still smokes cigarettes." I remember when we were little kids hiding in the alley, smoking cigarettes, thinking we were old, old men.

It was bugging me out. I realized for the first time how a lot of behavior that we associate with being a man is actually childish.

So I started looking at people my age, twenty-six years old, and comparing them to younger people and older people, checking out where they were at in their life.

I soon realized that age has nothing to do with it. It's a state of mind. You can be seventy years old and still not be a man. Or you can come to the realization of what it means to be a man at a very early age.

There is an interesting book out by author Susan Faludi, *Stiffed: The Betrayal of the American Man,* in which she argues that men have been compromised and have too much pressure on them to become men.

I think the pressure's needed. There's really a lot of men out there that are acting real immature. Smoking or drinking or any particular behavior doesn't necessarily make you immature. But your attitude and the way you conduct yourself does. I realize that the pressure to act like "a man" is there. But it's a state of mind, a way of thinking, and changing into a more responsible "man" is just a matter of attitude adjustment.

The guidelines, in my mind, are simple. Be responsible for your actions. Be honest. Be true. Treat others with respect. And in particular, don't lie and beat around the bush. I find myself telling my partner, Run, "Don't treat me like a kid. I'm not twelve anymore, and neither are you. Tell me what's on your mind. Speak up like a man!" And I'll do the same.

I think society has lost its way when it comes to meeting my definition of manhood. Youth today don't really see what I would define as "men."

When I was growing up, I looked to my father. He worked all his life. Left Florida at age sixteen and came to New York by himself. I look at my father, like, he's a man! He's not constantly smoking and drinking and partying. His whole life was mostly working to take care of his wife and his household.

But the generation that came after him? Oh my God. The

father figure is missing, and it seems like the mothers have taken over.

When I was growing up, there were men all around me. I noticed that my friends from those families that didn't have men are the ones that are in jail for life. They didn't have men in their lives. And maybe that explains why today, people who are twenty-eight and thirty years old are so immature.

I'm not saying that having a strong male in your life will cure all your problems. After all, I can point to myself as an example. But it does give you a compass that you can refer to at some point. When I finally came to this realization, I could look at my father and see the way a strong man leads his family.

Today, with the lack of fathers in so many households, and the lack of maturity of the males that actually are around, I'd say maybe 30 percent of American men can say they are really taking care of business.

We don't really need statistics and polls to back that up. Just open your newspaper. You'll see countless stories of child neglect, abusive behavior, irresponsible behavior. But hardly anything about the 30 percent who are quietly going about their lives, the rock-solid foundation of civilization.

The thing is, you don't have to put a lot of pressure on yourself to be "the man." Just try to be a better person. I don't agree with the old saying To be The Man you have to beat The Man.

No. Be the best you can be. Don't make it a contest. If there is a man you must beat, it's that man inside you that's luring you away from responsibility. Everybody's so busy trying to be better than the next man, they overlook their own development.

Instead of stepping on each other, pushing each other down, dividing ourselves as we claw our way to the top, creating winners and losers, let's all of us be men together and make things move.

Even with the lack of fathers in some homes, I think there are certain celebrities who are trying to make things better.

I look at Denzel Washington. He's a very big star. He's married, he's got four kids, he does his movies, he doesn't do anything negative, at least anything that the general public knows about.

I would say I like Denzel. He does three movies, but then he goes with his wife and kids on vacation.

In my son's case, I'm trying to keep my celebrity away from his life. I want him to be able to look at me like he'll look at another kid's father who isn't famous. I want him to always say, "My daddy. My daddy's strong." Or "My daddy reads to me." I don't want him thinking my celebrity status is what makes me.

Maybe he won't have to deal with it too much longer. I'm finding it harder and harder to be a performer as I get older. Whatever everyone thinks is so important about what I've done before, I'm telling them it isn't. I'm at the point where I'm a man, dammit.

I take inspiration from something Chuck D said on one of his albums, "I'm a man!" He said. "I don't care what people think about me, 'cause I'm a man."

Yeah, I started rapping and this is my career, show business. But I'm a man, dammit. I'm going home. I'm leaving for better things.

They don't give you any awards for acting like a man. Quite the opposite. I think the more immature and foolish you act, the more you're going to be hailed in show business. When you're a man, they don't want to hear from you. They don't want to hear what you're saying. They don't want to be around you.

When I lament the lack of leadership in my generation, one of the things I point to is the lack of positive, inspirational records. There's no one speaking like a man who is the same age as the prime audience for the music, or is one of the young producers and rappers making most of it.

Not to sound like an old man, but it was different for my generation. I had KRS-One and Public Enemy talking in my ear. Chuck D was twenty-five when he started.

Chuck D was my peer and I could relate to him. But he wasn't talking about what he had, the women and wine. He was talking like a man, talking about responsibility.

"We can do it," he said. "Just grow up! Wake up!" That's lacking in this generation. You can't show me one record that's doing it.

No one wants that responsibility. Everybody's too busy getting high and partying and thinking just because money is being made, everything's all right. But it's a total lie.

I know what you're thinking at this point. What is this man going to say to his son about drugs and other excesses?

I don't think I'm going to preach to him. We'll deal with these things together.

It's really different now from when I was growing up. I can give him the benefit of what I was going through in the sense that I can tell him about it.

But the situations he will face are far different than what I went through. That's the nature of society. It's moving too fast for any two generations to have much in common.

Someone once asked me why I didn't share my experiences with Biggie and Tupac about how to handle fame. And the answer is because I wasn't really dealing with what they were dealing with. When I was coming up, it was something different. Yes, there are similarities, and we can all point them out. But different is different.

The best thing I can do for my son is to grow up with him. That way, I'll have a better understanding of what he faces as he tries to grapple with problems. In a sense, I'll try to be his homey, rather than his *father*, with all the barriers and boundaries that implies.

In my opinion, a lot of people are messed up in the world because their parents are always trying to relate through what they went through. That misses the point, and the young person knows it. That solution leaves the young person struggling to cope with things on their own, and that's like flipping a coin—they can get lucky and make the right choices, or guess wrong and go in the opposite direction.

We've all heard fathers and mothers using that time-honored phrase, "When I was young, this is what was happening in the park, and that's why you can't do that."

"But Dad, that's not happening in the park no more."

"No, it's the same thing."

Hey, I see things all the time. When I go on the road now and I look at other groups—everyone from Snoop Dogg to Limp Bizkit—they all have their girls and associates, they all are in the record business, they are all Americans.

But similar situations? No. So that's why I'm not going to try to live my son's life for him.

That's not to say that there aren't things and situations I wouldn't want to prevent him from going through. When it comes to things like premarital sex and drugs and alcohol, I'd try my best to keep him away from that.

The best way to do that is show them an area that's better, more fun, more exciting, more positive. Offer alternatives, rather than just saying no, don't do that. As we've seen, that doesn't work.

I want to be able to hang with my son and have my son say, "Dad, take me here." That's a relationship built on confidence, rather than prevention.

I hope my son's in a good environment. He's still young, but by seven or eight, he's going to be facing things that I didn't experience until I was about eleven or twelve, and in some cases, things a lot of kids won't experience until their late teen years. That's the nature of our speeded-up society. The more you're exposed to all sorts of things, the faster you'll have to decide how to deal with them.

My wife tries to keep my son away from things. Like excessive television watching. She thinks it pollutes him.

I, on the other hand, try to let him watch it so he can understand that certain things are out there.

Right now, he loves *Blue's Clues,* but he's getting into action movies and things like that.

It's all one big wonder to him. When he sees an explosion on television, it's like, "Ohh, man!" or "Wow!" It's just starting to dawn on him that people might be injured or killed from it. He laughs if he sees the cartoon character fall on his face or get smacked. It's funny now but he is starting to understand what's going on.

That's the innocence of childhood. Whether he hears Lil' Kim, a really graphic rapper, or his dad, it's all the same to him. He just runs and gets his toy microphone to emulate the excitement of it, but he is beginning to know what the lyrics are.

That's why, as I mentioned before, I wish rappers would present things that show growth. Guys who sold crack and now have a record deal are still acting as though they're still partying in the ghetto with a bunch of their crew, as a way to show that they remember where they came from. But they're not showing that they worked hard to get over that mentality that keeps so many people imprisoned in poverty, with no alternative but a life of crime.

Back in the day, when you saw LL Cool J, Run-DMC, the Fat Boys, you wanted to become somebody like that. Nowadays it's a contest, who can be badder than the next guy. It's not enough to be like Biggie or Tupac—you gotta be rougher than them.

Don't take this as a call for censorship. There's a place for everything, and I would encourage people who really want that sort of music to seek it out.

But you can't walk into Blockbuster Video and buy a triple X movie.

I think that's the way it should be for records. Right now, a seven-year-old girl could walk into the store and buy a Lil' Kim album. That's not right.

Can they go to Blockbuster or Tower and buy *Debbie Does Dallas* or *Deep Throat?* Can they go to 7-Eleven and buy *Penthouse* or *Playboy?* No.

So I don't think they should do that with music. If they can't do it with movies or *Penthouse* or *Playboy,* why are we letting them do it with music?

I think you draw the line with age. You have to be a responsible adult in order to sample things that are intended for a mature audience.

That's not censorship. These kids are dealing with genocide and homicide and all kinds of things in their everyday lives. We don't need to reinforce the perception that these things are all right by encouraging them in popular entertainment available to everyone.

I think society has generally agreed that there needs to be some form of social order, some restrictions on the way people behave. Anything else and we'd be back several centuries, when you would take what your application of brute force permitted you to take.

I don't think it's asking too much to require subjects that require mature consideration to be restricted to mature adults.

An older man was driving me the other day to an appointment. "My kids love you guys," he was saying. "I've seen your albums in the house. But I don't like the stuff out there today. Some of that stuff is just too extreme."

Someone once told me the rappers are like the crack game of the eighties. You got these little drug cartels, rap is the product, and they're vying for space. That's why if I rhyme about you on the record, you're taking it seriously, because I'm dissing your territory. You're dissing the kingpin. And it's that mentality.

All the real essence of the art and music is getting lost.

It's not going to end anytime soon because right now it has a foundation. We're building a generation of people who aren't being exposed to a better vision, and their more destructive instincts are being reinforced by popular culture.

They're saying it's okay to lead this lifestyle. I say they're leading people off a cliff.

The Big Time

There's nothing like being on top in life. You're constantly surrounded by people who want to do things for you and with you. You're ushered into the VIP areas, you're introduced to all the right people. You're given priority clearance to do whatever you wish, whenever you wish.

But the true test of someone's character is how they act when things aren't going so well.

The MTV Video Music Awards are a good example of that from my own career. Because of the power and influence that the channel exerts on the music industry, not to mention the cache that comes with being one of the biggest influences on popular culture, MTV's awards ceremony and after party is the hottest one of the year in the entertainment business. It's like you're automatically certified as being cool if you're on the guest list.

Naturally, there's a large demand for tickets. Besides the record companies, there's advertisers, friends of the network, assorted celebrities, the musicians' entourages and handlers, and a few people who sneak in as contest winners.

Out of a universe of millions of people who want tickets, there's usually about six thousand seats available.

Maybe two or three years ago, I couldn't get tickets to get in there. We weren't hot on the charts, our record company wasn't creating any heat in the industry, and we didn't have anything really going on. In short, I couldn't do nothing for nobody.

But in 1999, Kid Rock was extremely hot on the charts, in large part because he represented a lot of what we had done. And now he's scheduled to appear on the show, and his whole performance was based around Run-DMC. It was like a medley of our songs, including our biggest hit, "Walk This Way." And suddenly we were on the guest list.

When we arrived, we pulled up in a limo. We just wanted to get out and go in, but no, the coordinators of the event wanted us to ride up in the limo and make a grand appearance on the red carpet. Hey, it's their show, and we're guests, so we agreed to it.

So we get out and take the walk up the red carpet, and all the MTV veejays and fashion models and flashbulbs were popping and everyone was staring and cheering.

And we got about halfway up this thing and I don't know why, I got this feeling, sort of indescribable, but I started saying to myself, "I don't want to be here."

I don't know why it came to me. But I looked at Run and I said, "I gotta tell you something. You don't know what I am thinking." He was probably thinking I'm going to say one of my jokes, because we always do stupid jokes.

Sort of on the order of, "What if I run over there and bash some celebrity in the face, what would the press think?" Okay, yeah, it's sick, but you have to think how surreal it is for some guys from Queens to be surrounded by all this.

I wanted to tell him that. But then I said, "Nah, this is something I gotta keep to myself." I'll share it with you now.

You know, I like a lot of the people there, the Ricky Martins and all of those kinds of acts. God bless them, they are talented and I applaud them for working hard and getting to where they've gotten in life. But a large part of the phoniness surrounding the whole event stems from the excitement surrounding them. They haven't really earned that kind of pandemonium.

The real people that I want to be around are the Sheryl Crows and the Bob Dylans and the Eric Claptons. Half the time they aren't even on these shows. They are too busy doing important, creative, brilliant stuff. They're making art, and they're doing it over a long stretch of time. Those are the people we should be going crazy over.

Me and Run were standing there saying, "Dag, we couldn't even get tickets last year." And now everyone is catering to us left and right.

What made it a unique experience for me was that everybody kept saying, "You guys are so easy to work with, y'all don't want nothing." And it was true. We were just there to do our performance.

I really don't like the fact that this was the year to treat us special. I wasn't any more special at that moment than I had been those two or three years before. I don't think a person deserves anything just because they are doing something that is interesting to the masses right now. I think people should carry respect for others regardless.

Once you're introduced to a person, I think you should always carry respect for that person. But that's not the entertainment industry. You don't really see it as a fan, but everything in the whole entertainment industry is built on phoniness.

It's akin to when the emperor or an elected official comes into the room. It's a courtesy friendliness. I felt that a lot back there.

Now, don't take this as a knock on MTV. They've always treated my group well. But I've always liked VH1 more. You look at MTV at what's happening this month. It's who's hot now, who's sold ten million this month. But next month they'll be gone.

VH1 is about the music. And that's what I've always wanted to be about.

Well, there is one exception to us being all about the music. There was a time we were getting so big—thanks to our album *Raising Hell*—that a mainstream corporation decided that this ghetto-bred music was safe for the rest of America's feet.

I'm talking, of course, about Adidas, a piece of footwear that Run-DMC is associated with to this day.

What Michael Jordan was to Nike, Run-DMC was to Adidas. It's funny that it turned out that way. In the history of rock 'n' roll, it's always been looked down on to be associated with a product. A lot of people wouldn't tour if there was sponsorship, and for a time, they certainly wouldn't let their music be associated with something as common as a commercial.

Honestly, we didn't start out with a commercial deal in mind. It was just part of our regular gear that we wore around Hollis when we were kids. And if you look at the lyrics of the song, we didn't really talk so much about how we loved the shoes— although we did—but about where we were and what we were doing while we were wearing them:

> My Adidas! Walked through concert doors
>   and roamed all over coliseum floors
> I stepped onstage at Live Aid
>   all the people gave and the poor got paid.

It was 1986, and we started our *Raising Hell* tour with a show at Madison Square Garden that April. Just before we hit the road, the album started gaining momentum, and word reached the Ad-

idas company that one of the hottest groups in America was selling their shoes.

Adidas finally sent out their representative, this guy named
Angelo Anastasio, to check out these Run-DMC guys. He couldn't
have picked a better show to attend. Here we are in our hometown, a crew of our most die-hard fans celebrating a real hot
album with us.

We started the chant—"Hold your Adidas in the air!"—and
it seemed like the whole Garden put their Adidas in the air. Angelo saw all this and his eyes were bugging out. After the show,
he came backstage and vowed to get us a deal. Thus began our
long association with the company, one that continues to this day.

Of course, as much as we loved certain clothes, we also
pointed out our problems with gear that we didn't like. You'll
remember a line I wrote for "Rock Box" that Run said on the
record: "Calvin Klein's / no friend of mine / don't want nobody's
name on my behind."

Never heard from my favorite brand, Lee jeans, though. . . .

One of our career highlights wasn't about the music either. It was
about showing up to represent the fact that musicians from all
genres of the business cared about human suffering.

We were on the road in 1985 for the second Fresh Fest tour
when we got a call that we had to fly to Philadelphia first thing
the next morning for Live Aid, the concert held to raise money
for the victims of a famine in Ethiopia. It was to be the show of
shows—sixty-one of rock's biggest acts performing for seventeen
hours in London and Philadelphia to raise money for African
famine relief.

I was aware of Bob Geldof and his efforts to organize the
show, but I hadn't been following the developments, particularly
since no one had asked us to be a part of it.

As it turned out, the fact that no one had asked us was the
most controversial part of the entire show. People said that there

were only something like three black performers initially asked to appear on the show. When he was questioned about it, Geldof created even more controversy by claiming that everyone on the Billboard charts had been contacted, implying that we and others had turned him down.

To this day, as far as I know, we weren't invited. I've heard that we asked about it when the concert was first announced, but were told the slots had been filled.

But Bill Graham, the concert promoter, had taken a look at the show's lineup and realized there were few African American performers. He personally requested Run-DMC to be on the bill. Thus, we dropped everything and made it a point to head to Philadelphia.

You have to remember what it was like for rap at the time. We were playing coliseums to our fans, but it had yet to become a mass-media, top-of-the-charts phenomenon for a lot of people. We were really new to the world. But that doesn't excuse the lack of R & B or other performers.

In the end, Graham and others stepped in and invited Ashford and Simpson, the Four Tops, Billy Ocean, and a lot of other black performers who were doing well on the charts. That settled that issue, and it was back to focusing on the real problem, starving people.

It wasn't until we were being briefed about Live Aid that the magnitude of what we were going to be a part of hit us: "Whoa! That's big."

So, even though we were tired as hell from a show the night before in Savannah, Georgia, everyone headed to Philadelphia. I remember everyone around us was flipping out about how big a deal it was. We were too tired to argue.

Let me tell you: it was big. I mean, you could arguably say it was the biggest show in rock 'n' roll history. Check out the lineup: Black Sabbath, Sade, Sting, U2, the Beach Boys, Tina Turner, Queen, Elton John, The Who, Bob Dylan, Led Zeppelin, Madonna, Paul McCartney. And, of course, Run-DMC. It doesn't get any bigger.

The Big Time

We arrived at JFK Stadium in Philadelphia, this big old coliseum that looked like something out of Roman times. Everyone was treating us like royalty because we had Bill Graham touting us.

They had a dressing room with our name on it, everything first class all the way. Mr. Graham came over to us before we went on to thank us for coming. He was really cool.

Backstage was kind of interesting. All the celebs were asking for autographs for their children.

It was well over one hundred degrees that July day and really humid in Philadelphia; I mean, sticky in the way that the South gets sometimes. People were passing out all over the place in the crowd. It was a hectic show. We had like twenty minutes to set up our turntables, and then we had three songs to make an impact, a total of about six minutes onstage, all told. Scheduling was that tight, what with that many acts.

Mix that in with how new rap was to the mostly white audience, and you have a tough crowd to work.

So they put us on right near the start of the show, in the blinding daylight.

That was by far one of the biggest crowds we ever performed in front of, and still is to this day. Over one hundred thousand people, plus a worldwide audience watching on TV.

What's it like to work something that big? Actually it didn't feel good, I tell you that. There wasn't any connection with the crowd. Even though we had been playing coliseums, it felt like we were a million miles away. At Live Aid, the stage was up high and the people that were right in front of me were still far away, extending in a sea of people all the way to the back of the stadium. I felt so distant from the crowd.

We did "King of Rock" and something else. I don't even remember making eye contact with one person in the crowd.

Before we knew it, the show was over. And we were on our way back out on the road, back to the intimate confines of the nation's coliseums. We had learned what it was like to put on a show before a million people. And although it wasn't like we tore the place apart, I learned a lesson from Live Aid about the responsibility that is placed upon me as a performer, particularly when the eyes of the world are on me.

It's hard, sometimes, to be totally aware of what's happening in the real world when you're caught up in your own tour.

We traveled from town to town, doing interviews, following schedules for soundchecks and whatnot. But then another cause came to us: Little Steven Van Zandt, of Bruce Springsteen's E Street Band, contacted us to be on his antiapartheid record and video, decrying the performers who played at Sun City, a South African resort that banned nonwhite guests.

I honestly hadn't been following the politics there. I was just dumb to the factor. At the same time, we were always a group that was willing to speak out about social and political issues, making records like "It's Like That" and "Hard Times" and stuff like that. We were a message group. So I got educated real fast when he contacted us.

Little Steven knew how important it was to have the hip-hop camp with him on this one. So he recruited us, Melle Mel, Kurtis Blow, the whole hip-hop thing.

Once we got into the project, I was stunned. "Wow, this is what's going on?" It was incredible to me that a place with that much money, such a beautiful place physically, could contain such an ugly policy as apartheid. Black people couldn't vote, travel freely, own land in certain parts of the country—I mean, it was slavery.

The idea of the project was to draw attention to the United Nations' call for a worldwide sports and cultural boycott of South Africa until it changed its policies. It also spotlighted the racism that exists in all cultures.

Little Steven decided making a record and video about Sun City was the perfect way to let the public know which performers had played the resort—and the list included one of my heroes, Elton John, as well as Frank Sinatra, Tina Turner, Linda Ronstadt, and Rod Stewart—and the people who turned down the money.

People like Stevie Wonder and Gladys Knight. The song's chorus was "I ain't gonna play Sun City."

Because of everyone's schedules, we recorded our contributions to the record, which was called *Sun City,* separately. But we did gather for the accompanying video, and that was some of the most fun I've had with other performers.

For the video, all the groups put aside all their animosity and jealousy and new school versus old school rivalries, and got down and had some fun.

At the video shoots, about fifty artists came to Harlem and to Washington Square Park in Greenwich Village to show support for the cause.

We were all there just laughing and having fun. I don't know why, but it just happened that way. The Fat Boys, Run-DMC, Melle Mel, Kurtis Blow, Scorpio, and even Bruce Springsteen, interacting with each other, Bruce cracking jokes, everyone laughing. That was a good time, the way most fans probably think it is all the time in music.

Unfortunately, making music and being an entertainer isn't that way all the time. In fact, a lot of times things veer into territory that's anything but funny.

We were out on tour in August 1986 on our *Raising Hell* tour with five other groups. We had not had much trouble on the tour. But then we arrived in Los Angeles.

Los Angeles was a strange place to people from New York. We knew not to wear red or blue to L.A. because of the gang situation, but we really didn't understand the mentality out there, the stone-cold gangsta life that was brewing.

We knew there were gangs out there. We had gangs in New York, the Black Skulls, the Savage Skulls, the Seven Immortals. But they were just street gangs who wore colors. It wasn't on the level it was in L.A. We didn't know about the drive-bys and didn't know about the gang signs.

It's funny. For a time, if a rapper flicked his hands the wrong way, the press would write, "They're throwing gang signs in the video." I don't know about others, but we didn't know about any of this. We just knew there were two gangs that are out there that are really big. Don't wear red, don't wear blue, and you might not get shot.

Even Chuck D of Public Enemy, the man who commands the most respect of any rapper on the planet, was told to wear black when he came to L.A. It's a neutral color. Wear a black Raiders jacket and hat, everyone is told. That's why N.W.A and all the other guys picked up on that. It was the neutral street hood color. But we knew it was real crazy.

We had actually been spending a lot of time in L.A. on things related to our careers. When we had some downtime, we'd go into Crip territory and they'd rush our car and love us. And we'd go into the Blood territory and they'd rush our car and love us.

This is when rock cocaine was so big. We'd drive through and they'd run at the car with the drugs. "Yo! What y'all want? Oh, shoot! That's Run-DMC." 'Cause we would always just drive around the hood and go get beers from the local stores. So we knew it was volatile, especially from the people who lived there. And so, we headed to Long Beach for our show knowing there might be trouble.

What happened was, about 12:30 we went to Long Beach Arena for soundcheck. It was already getting packed out in the parking lot.

We went there, did the soundcheck, and the drivers, a couple of the young guys driving the vans and limos, said, "Yo. It's going to be ill today. I'm telling ya, it's goin' to be ill today." There was just that vibe in the air. I don't think the police really expected it. I mean, they had the usual police with the horses and stuff out there. But it didn't look like it was that much more than usual.

But after we came back to the arena that night, it was off the hook. I mean, crazy, mass police presence around the arena. Something was in the air, a vibe that things were about to go off.

The Big Time

When we got inside the arena, Whodini was on the way out from the backstage area. We gave them the usual high fives and wishes for a good show. So they continued on out and we headed into our dressing room.

About three minutes or so later, Vanessa Williams, her manager, and her bodyguard came running into our dressing room. Vanessa was crying and almost hysterical.

"We don't know what's going on out there," her manager said. "It's crazy out there!"

Our road manager, Lyor Cohen, came in. "Oh my God," he said. "They're killing each other out there."

We learned later what was up. According to reports, about two hundred members of local gangs went running through the crowd while Whodini was performing. They had knives and chair legs that they had broken off, and used them against the rival gang members.

We're looking at each other, wondering what we should do. Then the arena's head of security came into our dressing room. He was sweating like crazy, his eyes bugging out with a fearful look. "Y'all got to stay in this dressing room!" he shouted.

That was it. We didn't know what was happening, but we weren't going to take a chance. Me and Jay started taking chairs and ripping them apart to get the chair legs. Whatever was going on outside in that hallway, if they came in here, they're going to catch some knocks before they get anything off.

We soon learned exactly how bad it was outside. Whodini came into our dressing room and gave us the details. They had stopped in the middle of a song and put the house lights up. From the stage, they could see that the arena was out of control.

"We went out there and they just started fighting, man," said Jalil of Whodini. "We were in the middle of our song and I looked up and I seen a guy come off the top balcony down to the floor. I know he gotta be dead."

He said the crowd just started picking up chairs and anything they could find to throw or hit people over the head with. Standing onstage, they watched as a crew of red ran up into this section of the place, then a crew of blue ran up into that section. Jalil said everybody, girls and all, just started fighting.

The scary thing was that the fighting wasn't confined to one particular section or group of combatants, as happens in most fights that break out at concerts. You know, someone gives some-one a shove, his friends jump in, that sort of thing.

This time, it wasn't one isolated incident where security and the police could swarm in and stop it. The whole place exploded at once.

You had to believe that the gangs had come there that night for the showdown. I mean, none of the acts on the bill had any-thing violent in their lyrics or reputations. I mean, we had Run-DMC, Whodini, LL Cool J, whose big hit at the time was, ironically, "I Need Love." We might have looked like our peers in the streets, but we weren't gangbangers.

Well, we were held captive in our own dressing room for at least two hours while the battle raged outside. We didn't know what was happening, but every now and then, someone from se-curity would come in and tell us that things hadn't stopped, and deliver what was mostly bad news. "They're laying out every-where," was one particular message I remember.

It was tense inside that room. We didn't know what was going on outside our door, wondering if at any minute we'd be fighting for our lives.

Finally security came in and told us we could leave. When we walked out of the dressing room, we saw the battleground. I mean, it was a wrecked arena. There was blood, jewelry, pocket-books, sneakers, jackets, food, all over the place, randomly dropped in the panic. I mean, we saw metal shards where they ripped the seats out of the floor.

We headed back to our hotel and turned on the news. Every-thing was blaring about the gang fight. Most of the reports in-sisted it was all about rap. "Rap causes gang fight. Rap this, rap that."

Reports the next day said 45 were injured out of the crowd of 14,500.

We knew that we were going to have to talk about this, so we held a meeting to go over what we were going to say. We had a show scheduled for the Hollywood Palladium the following night, but that was quickly canceled. We didn't want to have anything else go down in Los Angeles.

Despite everything, we didn't think that it was going to be more than something we'd have to deal with for a couple days. After all, we get to the next town, explain what happened, and it's over. On to the next. It's a problem in Los Angeles.

But this was bigger than something that happened locally. Because it was rap music that the people supposedly came out to see, it became a national issue.

At 2:00 A.M., we were contacted about appearing on ABC TV the next morning. We had to get up at like 5:00 A.M. to get to their studios. And we wound up not only defending our name—because, after all, we were the headliners—but rap music itself.

A researcher at Michigan State University was quoted in *USA Today* tying rap music to the gang problem. Rap music, he said, "incites a bad attitude. The hostility is there, kids identify with it and it's a marriage made in hell."

Tipper Gore, the wife of then senator and later vice president Al Gore, was very active in the music community at the time. She was head of something called the Parents' Music Resource Center, a group of politically connected wives who staged media campaigns against rock and rap music.

Tipper Gore agreed with the Michigan researcher. "You have angry, disillusioned, unloved kids," said Gore. "They unite behind heavy metal or rap music and the music says it's OK to beat people up."

Huh? Me singing about eating Mom's macaroni and cheese in Hollis? Telling kids to stay in school?

But it's an issue that wouldn't go away.

Does rap music cause gang violence? I heard that question

that day and for years afterward. Somehow, my talking on a microphone over some beats was the cause of all sorts of social problems, according to some people who didn't listen to my records.

Worse, everything started to be blended together. This was the height of the Crips and Bloods in L.A., the crack plague, the movie *Colors,* which saw some violence in neighborhood theaters when it premiered.

In the minds of the media, it all had a common root: rap music. Instead of doing a press conference about our tour coming to town, we spent the whole conference defending ourselves. You know, all about how the town fathers should allow us to come in, and they shouldn't worry about anything.

I remember the first words out of our mouths at most press conferences for the next three or four years was usually, "The thing that happened in L.A. wasn't because . . ."

So we had a dual role. We had to promote our careers and calm the fears of a nation worried that music was going to cause all sorts of problems. If you look at footage of what the early days of rock 'n' roll were like, with all sorts of "leagues of decency," you'll see the parallels.

We had to patiently explain that no, rap music doesn't cause people to tear up the arena. Yes, sometimes incidents do happen at shows, outside shows, on the way to shows. Just like they do when people attend sporting events, the opera, or go grocery shopping. It's called life.

If you buy a Run-DMC album, you will not hear anything that incites violence in any way. You go buy Whodini, they're singing about how the freaks come out at night. And LL Cool J, he's just bragging about how good he is on the microphone, but his main hit is a ballad, "I Need Love." Or go buy the Fat Boys. You might blame them for making you hungry, but you won't go out and pound on your neighbor.

It seems like rock 'n' roll—but particularly music by black artists—has been targeted for years, accused of promoting everything from promiscuity to violence. As a result, our early shows had more police presence than you'll see at any events of similar size and scope. It wasn't that more stuff happened at our shows. It was the perception that something could happen. And it's statements like Tipper Gore's that created that atmosphere.

I had some qualms with some members of the media who tried to pin the whole Long Beach Arena incident on us.

On the whole, though, I'd say the media has portrayed Run-DMC fairly well over the years. I have no major beefs.

Everybody gets so mad with the media, but they're only doing their job. Regardless if they're reporting dirty stuff. What amazes me is how people get mad at the media for hyping it up, like they did with the whole East Coast rap scene versus West Coast rap scene. But there were a lot of other people adding fuel to that fire.

As far as Long Beach, I may not have liked everything that came out, but when I look back, they were only trying to figure it out. It was when rap was just entering the mainstream, and it was pretty easy to confuse the music with the whole urban cultural scene, including the good people with the bad.

What they should have written at the time—and what, thankfully, most outlets know now—is that white people, black people, Hispanic people, Japanese people, nice people, good people, drug dealers, gangbangers from L.A., drug sellers from my neighborhood in Queens and the Bronx and Manhattan, all liked my music, and rap in general.

But that doesn't mean that every time there's a concert, something's going to be set off. I hate to say it, but it seems pretty obvious that a lot of the reporting was slanted because it was a riot by black gangbangers at a black entertainer's show. It's easy for the nation's largely white reporters to blame it all on the collective "they."

And we were the most visible scapegoat as the leaders of the rap movement.

As an outgrowth of all this negative attention on our group and our art, we became involved in anticensorship organizations that were battling the PMRC and other conservative groups. I appeared at several press conferences. I told anyone who would pay attention that they should merely stop, look, listen, and learn. There was nothing to be afraid of, despite the messages that some people were putting out.

Even with all our efforts, there was some fallout. Rap took the heat for the actions of the gangs, and consequently, we had a tough time getting reasonably priced insurance to cover our shows over the next few years, which made it hard to get into the big venues.

What happened in Long Beach was different from what happened recently at Woodstock. But there are similiarities that I'd like to share with you.

I believe you have a responsibility to your audience as a performer that goes beyond entertainment. For the moment that you are up there on the stage, you are the king, you are the god, and, often, you are the law. If you accept the power that the microphone gives you, then you have to accept the responsibility.

The music of Korn, Limp Bizkit, Kid Rock, and others in that sort of rock/rap genre is usually built around an energetic, rebellious, all-out, I-don't-give-a-whatever-about-your-law mentality and performance. That's what makes that music what it is.

It also makes it easy for things to spiral out of control. At Woodstock, the crowd was on the verge of anarchy. They were hot, tired, wired, and ready for an evening featuring some high energy. In short, it was like dry tinderbrush, ready to be set off.

And here comes Limp Bizkit, the kings of setting things off, carrying a book of matches in their attitude toward the situation.

At Long Beach, the acts didn't encourage anybody to do anything but have a good time. Yeah, we were hoping that the crowd was enthusiastic, ready to party, energetic. But we weren't encouraging the crowd to exhibit that behavoir with a gang war. I mean, LL Cool J's big hit at the time was "I Need Love." These weren't calls to battle that the crowd was hearing.

At Woodstock, Fred Durst brought the crowd beyond "Let's party!" In effect, he told them, "It's okay to be crazy."

Worse, he didn't learn anything from his Woodstock experience. When we were in Hartford, Connecticut, on the Family Values tour, there were more fireworks from Limp Bizkit, and more ugly scenes. Apparently, some bands don't give a damn about the potential for trouble or don't care about their fans. The artist is the center of all that energy. It's one thing to tell the people to let it all loose, but letting it all loose can also mean you're being careful, courteous, cautious, and responsible for everyone around you.

I mean, there have been a hundred times that Run-DMC has been onstage and a fight broke out and we stopped it. Jay will grab the no, mic and come to the front and say, "Yo! Stop it! We ain't going to have none of that shit here!" And we'll talk to them and they'll understand it. And then we're able to complete our show.

What you don't do is go up there and say, "Fuck the police." You *can* go up there and say, "Come on down!" When we do a concert in a big coliseum and they have seats on the floor, we tell everybody, forget about the seats. Get up! This ain't no library! You ain't at the opera! And they'll all bunch their way up to the front and they'll all fill the floor.

The way we do it, the cops don't mind because it's done in a nice, safe, good-times way. But when you go out there and say fuck the police and fuck the security, that means the fans can lose it because their king said so.

Along those lines, I don't think it's always the public that puts entertainers up on too high a platform.

I think that entertainers put *themselves* up on too high a platform.

Look at Michael Jackson. The way he leads his life and what he allows the public to see pushes him further and further away from society. The only reason he can't go into any store he wants is that he makes it into a big event when he goes anywhere.

On the one hand, if that's what he wants, you have to give

him credit. Regardless of whether or not he has another hit, he will still be a celebrity because of the mystery that surrounds him.

Whether or not he has hits, he's always going to be Michael.

I am the type of guy that will allow anyone into my space. I'm never nervous when I'm out eating in a restaurant and have to deal with fans who come up seeking to say hello and get an autograph. I've never said, "It's kind of disrespectful. Can't you see I'm eating?"

A lot of stars doing that. "I ain't signing nothing right now." In fact, Whitney Houston dissed one of my relatives who merely came up to her and asked for an autograph.

The result? My relative said, "I'll never buy her record again." Just by shunning that person, you're putting yourself on a pedestal.

I'm talking about having respect for your fellow human beings as humans. That allows you, even if one hundred million people are standing in line for autographs, to go wherever you wish. If you give others their space, they will reciprocate.

I've often wondered what people are reacting to when they see someone famous.

On the one hand, thanks to television and radio interviews, as a celebrity you've been a part of their lives in their homes. They've seen you in their living rooms when they're at home relaxing, so you've become part of their lives.

So when they see you on the street, there's this bond between you. And a lot of people want to extend that bond a little further. That's understandable.

When you're onstage, it's a different situation. I believe they're reacting to a number of things. Some people sit there and sing the lyrics along with you. They're doing that in solidarity. They've sat in their rooms and listened to your records and have been inspired by the message of the song. Others are doing it for the fantasy. They want to be you, so they're projecting themselves into the stage situation.

Recently, I have begun to think that what they're reacting to is the notion that Run-DMC is something that represents some aspect of their lives. Maybe they heard our songs during a particular moment that was special, maybe it helped them through some times, maybe they had a great party where our music was played. And there we are, the living embodiment of that emotion, up there on the stage, performing in a somewhat intimate surrounding.

On another, scarier level, you have the person who believes that's the person that I love. That's God up there onstage. That's the living realization of everything that I want to express. That's when it can get a little out of control.

But most of the time, being a performer is a pretty nonthreatening and positive situation.

I had been having some problems with my vocal cords over the last few years from constantly performing. When I first was having problems, the bishop of my church was sympathetic to the problem but encouraged me to go out there even if my sound wasn't exactly what I would have liked it to be. He had what I believe is the proper perspective on performance.

"Go out there and continue doing the shows," he told me. "It's not that they just want to hear you do your record perfect. They want to see that that's really DMC that they heard on these records and tapes all these years."

After he told me that, I looked at our audience differently. We did Detroit shortly after that conversation, and when I looked out at the audience, I saw the reaction from the crowd. It wasn't so much that they cared about our particular performance that evening. It was just that we could bond and share a moment over the particular music that was being performed.

I looked out at the people, and saw their look of love and respect. "That's my man!" We were celebrating Run-DMC's essence at that moment, and each person was attaching their particular memories and feelings surrounding our music to that experience.

Yes, depending on the performer, it has something to do with you. Maybe some girls think, "That's the guy I want to marry and have sex with." And the guys: "That's my nigger up there! Yo!

That's my man!" But, in truth, it's more about celebrating along with some music, and each person's experiences when they heard that music plays into the atmosphere.

I think the whole lyrics/artist thing disappears right there. And if certain stars realized that, they'd be better off in their private lives.

As Run-DMC moved into the last two years of the 1980s and into the 1990s, we were struggling. I had my own physical and financial problems, as did Jay.

But Run was going through some particularly tough times as a result of our situation. From the high life of *Tougher than Leather,* a period when we were acclaimed as one of the top groups in the world, we had started to slide.

Fame can be like a drug. When the attention goes away, you can crash if you let it mean that much to you. Run took it hard. He talked about suicide but never could actually go through with it.

Later, he suffered a nervous breakdown. He subsequently gained a lot of weight and saw his marriage flounder.

There wasn't much any of us in the group could do. We were struggling with problems of our own, most of them the same ones as his.

But all of those troubles were put in perspective by something that came down after a tour stop in Cleveland.

It was a nice, sunny day in Hollis. I remember I was out driving in my car. It was after the *Back from Hell* tour, and I was looking forward to a nice, relaxing day.

Then my car phone rang. It was our road manager, Big D, and I could tell from the tone of his voice that something heavy was about to go down.

"Yo, D. Wassup with this girl in Cleveland that said Run raped her?"

The Big Time

I almost drove off the road.

"What?!!!!" This was unbelievable, but I knew Big D wasn't the type to kid around about something like this.

I didn't have much memory of Cleveland. We did a show there that night, one of thousands I've done in my career, and it wasn't particularly memorable. It was maybe two, three in the morning when we left town. I wasn't sure why we left that night, but we were driving everywhere at the time, so it didn't seem all that unusual to me. At any rate, I was tired from the show, so I didn't ask too many questions.

Run was flying home the next day, but we often traveled separately, so even that wasn't unusual.

I don't remember if I called Run that day, but I finally reached him on his phone when he was at Taco Bell with his kids. He thought it was so crazy that he couldn't believe it, and was just mad about having to go though the procedures of getting a lawyer, flying back to Cleveland to surrender, and the whole process. He knew he was innocent, so all he could focus on was the inconvenience of having to prove that.

Actually, after the initial shock, it didn't bother me all that much either. To me, it was just something that happened. Another bit of business, not something I was surprised at.

Once again, I can almost hear your surprise. I know it's hard for the average person to understand the life we lead. But in our world, strange things happen, and you just deal with them and move on. Even in a case like this, where it's much more serious than the everyday hassles.

Run met the girl the usual way. It's not hard to find out where we're staying in town when we're on the road. So after the show, there's usually a fair amount of people in the lobby of the hotel, waiting to say hello, get an autograph, or, in the case of certain women, a little more than that.

I guess they're waiting to be picked. And sometimes, they are. You can make your choice. Everybody's ripe for the picking. And that's like the usual set.

But clearly there's a danger in hooking up with a stranger.

Anybody could just say anything about you, and it's a classic he said/she said situation.

I don't know what happened with Run that night. I'm a loner. When I get offstage, I don't watch everyone's business.

The woman claimed Run took her to his hotel room and forced her to have oral sex with him.

I've known Run since kindergarten, and I knew he was no rapist. But would a jury in Cleveland believe this loudmouth, gold-chain-and-hat-wearing New York celebrity? That was the scary part to me. What if he's gotta do years?

I had seen what accusations could turn into. I know a guy who was a bodyguard. He was on tour and brought a girl back from the show to the hotel where they were staying.

The girl was pretty wild. From what he tells me, she gave it up to about three or four guys, then had sex with him.

But her father came to the hotel to get her, and all hell broke loose.

It was crazy. The girl voluntarily went to the hotel with him and voluntarily did what she did. But he was the only one charged, and he wound up serving ten years in prison. Ten years out of his life.

Run's case got attention in places that usually didn't give a damn about Run-DMC. One of our constant complaints in our career was that *Ebony* and *Jet* magazine, two of the most prominent black publications that always trumpet the triumphs of our community, never, ever put Run-DMC on their cover, despite all our firsts in the record industry.

Yet when Run's situation happened, they suddenly devoted a lot of space to him.

It was driving him crazy, and he was out there by himself. The press didn't even call me to answer any questions. Everywhere he went, he was confronted by it. On the plane ride back from Cleveland, Run was sitting in the first-class section of the airplane, surrounded by businessmen. He looks up at the movie screen, and they were showing an in-flight news program. There, displayed for everyone in the cabin, was his face as a member of Run-DMC, arrested and charged with rape.

Run's brother, Russell, got him the best lawyers he could find. His legal team decided that it would be best if me, Jay, and the rest of his posse didn't show up in court to support him. Instead, only his mother, father, brother, and the actual witnesses he would call were asked to come.

It was getting very scary during the trial. The girl made a convincing witness as she laid out her tale against Run. The prosecution seemed eager to paint him as a celebrity running wild, without any real regard for the rights of others. Very scary.

Thankfully, someone's conscience was touched by Run's plight. A friend of the woman's came forward in court and said she had told her once that she made up a similar tale about another man. The judge didn't even bother sending the case to the jury. He dismissed it with prejudice, which means the charges could never be brought again.

Of course, that wasn't the end of Run's nightmare. His marriage, which admittedly was already shaky, dissolved in the wake of the incident. Worse, everywhere he went, he had to talk about his ordeal in endless detail, defending himself again and again.

Although I won't say that he was treated totally unfairly by the media, I will point out that the accusations against him were given prominent play, but the acquittal was buried. Like with our incident in Long Beach, the atmosphere that something was Run-DMC's fault seemed to linger, particularly for Run.

There were some immediate changes on the road in the wake of Run's trial. "No girls in the dressing room or near it" was the order Run gave. It actually bothered our road crew, who were used to a lot of fine-looking women being around and available.

But that behavior lasted only a minute for our entourage. Soon, it was back to business as usual.

It's hard for people to learn. Like with the AIDS situation, everyone is frightened for a brief period, then moves on and reverts to their previous behavior.

The thing that's funny is that when you're doing it, you as the celebrity forget about it. I don't think about the ones that did it with me.

You know, you worry now when you go back to these towns. "Remember me?" That's like the big joke on the road. Me and Jay and Run, we always say that. "D, you be scared when you go to Tennessee and you think, 'Yeah, I slept with her one night.' " And you could go to L.A. with your wife and get, "Remember me in 1983?"

Like the other day, me and Run both got nervous when someone came up to us in a hotel lobby. This white girl came up and she had her video camera and her pictures—"In 1985, when y'all were with the Beasties, this and that, we hung out and I was up in the hotel"—all this stuff in front of the people standing around us.

Run's thinking, "She's going to say me or say D or Jay had done something really wild with her." But then she just launched into some long story about how she was hanging with Ad Rock and whatever. It was all innocent. She didn't even do nothing with them, just came up to do an interview for her high school.

But that's the price we pay for our past. Everyone that approaches us might have some score to settle. It's a fear we live with everyday.

Getting It Together

One of the hardest things I've ever had to do was talk about my life on the road with my wife, even though all of this happened before we had met.

When I finally laid it all out for her, she had a hard time understanding and got really mad at me. "How could you do this?"

She's right. How could I have done all of that? I guess my only rationale for it now is that I was young, caught up in the euphoria of being a celebrity that was creating something new. I didn't stop and think, but just gave in to my urges.

I regret a lot of my behavior. I should have listened to my

conscience and had the courage not to follow the crowd. Many times that inner voice told me, "No, you don't have to. That's not going to make you a man and you don't have to compete with anybody." But I gave in to the desire and the impulse and the urge, let it be stronger than my common sense.

After a lot of thinking, I figured out what had led me to that state. The temptations that I had dealt with reminded me of a situation in my neighborhood.

I had once been introduced to someone at a party, and I felt instant dislike from this person. No reason for it. Nothing was said. But we all know that feeling, that cold, harsh attitude that comes off some people.

I didn't say anything at the time, but it soon became so obvious that there was a problem that I had to discuss it with Run. I was like, "Why is this person playing me like this?" Just everything they said around me and at me was really hostile. And I couldn't figure it out.

This was back when I always wore my Run-DMC getup everywhere, and I had a Cadillac and a big Gucci rope chain, I had a Rolex on my arm.

Jack seemed to take my appearance anywhere in his vicinity as a personal affront. I remember him muttering to people, "He ain't nobody. Why he got to be here? Why you got to be with him? Who does he think he is?"

This person couldn't respect me. It was somebody that just hated me.

The feud—if we can call it that, since I never really responded to his insults—didn't end in any special way. He just lost the battle he had going on with himself. Whatever it was that didn't allow him to get past the fact that success had come to Darryl from the neighborhood, just ended.

I think what upset him wasn't me. He was upset at himself, jealous of what I represented.

In a strange sense, I think I was just like this person at one time. Only the person that I was jealous of was DMC, the imaginary creation that I had built up over the years. Thus, I had to live as large as I thought DMC should live.

In order to save myself, I had to get back to being Darryl McDaniels.

I think that there's just a point in life where you mature, and some people mature quicker than others. Some people are able to do it at seventeen and eighteen and not be depressed about it. Just go to work and come home and get up and drive the bus or do the UPS mail or whatever. Others, it takes until they get married, or achieve some success of their own.

I didn't mature until I was maybe twenty-eight years old. I had been acting like I was sixteen since I was sixteen, going through a lot of living in a short time. But I woke up to my responsibilities as a man when I came out of the hospital after suffering from pancreatitis.

But the real, most profound change of my life was my marriage. Meeting my wife caused me to just wake up the next day and discover that I no longer had the desire to be sixteen. It just clicked. I'm not going to be silly, not going to be loud, not going to run the red light. It's like my eyes were opened to the possibilities that lay within what the world calls maturity.

Maturity is not a matter of age. You've got old men who want to drive Corvettes.

Ideally, though, there are ways to act your age, even though that's not necessarily the same thing as being mature. Let me run them down for you and see if you don't agree with me.

At age twenty, I believe you should start to act like the adult that you are. Show some responsibility. Don't wait for Mom and Dad, your teachers, or your coworkers to bail you out of every situation. You're beginning to build the foundation for who you will be the rest of your life.

At age thirty, you should be really connecting the dots and putting a game plan into action. You should be able to easily make lists titled "I am comfortable with this" and "I am still dealing with that." But you should also be comfortable enough with your position in life to say, "I have arrived. This is who I am. I know what I have to do and I know how to deal with everybody else."

Projecting forward from my current age, at forty years old you should be able to understand everybody that is younger than you, and be able to respect everybody older than you, because everybody older than you is going to be looking for you to act a certain way at forty.

I've got to confess, I feel older than I am most of the time, which is a particular problem since I've been in the public eye so long. Everybody that's my age now wants me to be that young guy I was when I was eighteen. "Put the glasses back on. Where's the goatee? Where's the glasses?"

That's my burden. I want to build on who I am now and let them know I am no longer that eighteen-year-old DMC. I want them to take time out and respect me for who I am now. Don't diss me because I'm not what you're expecting me to be.

This may really surprise you, but I don't listen to rap anymore. I don't care about listening to more songs in the genre that I helped pioneer. Been there, done that. All I listen to now are English bands from the 1960s and 1970s, the Beatles, John Lennon, Pink Floyd, Elton John. I keep my radio on classic rock stations.

I'm comfortable with the transition I'm making in life. But it's not been as easy for my partners. Run is still acting like the guy that he once was, that eighteen-year-old who came off the streets of Hollis and became an international rap star. He wants success on the same terms. He still wants his respect and props from the street. I don't even care about that anymore.

But even Run is starting to concede a few things. The other day he said something that made me sit back. "D, I must be getting older, because I don't get the flow and these beats these guys are rapping over today. I mean, it is some of the blandest stuff." For him to admit that took a lot of courage, because it's a concession that he's more comfortable with something that isn't the absolute freshest thing of the moment.

I know I am older because what I want to hear is something new. I want to hear a message; I want to hear some vision. And I don't want you to resent me for wanting to change as I grow up.

Of course, I'll admit that some of the resentment that people may have as I try to change may be my fault, particularly as it relates to people who I deal with in my day-to-day interactions.

I can be a loner at times. In one case, with the Beastie Boys, I had a feeling a couple of them didn't care for me because of that.

Adam Horovitz and me were always cool. But Adam Yauch and Mike Diamond, I don't know. We always seemed like our relations were strained.

I never hung out with them when we were on the road or making movies together, so maybe they took that personally. It was nothing against them. Just went my own way.

Jay and Run would always go to the Beastie Boys' rooms on the road, smoke reefer with them, and write rhymes. They'd also go ride on their bus. Like I said, I never hung, but I don't hang with anybody. So maybe they thought I didn't like them, that I was too big for them.

Or maybe it was something else. Run told me once that they told him my rhymes were corny. I think he said it to kind of egg me on. He would say how they are going to finally tell me to my face how they really felt.

I used to play right into Run's hands, getting really upset at that prospect. How are they going to say that to me, when the whole reason they had this style is because of me? I mean, they've admitted it in their interviews.

Finally I wised up. None of the Beastie Boys ever came around and dissed me to my face. I don't know if they ever really said anything, or if Run was merely dogging me like he does.

King of Rock

I went to one of their concerts recently, and my wife said I should have seen the look on Adam Yauch's face when he saw me. He came over and hugged me and led me over to the side of the stage where we could watch the show.

That was wonderful, and I appreciated it. I don't really think they had a problem with me.

Lauryn Hill said something recently that struck me as a parallel to my situation with Run-DMC. She said her groupmates in the Fugees, Pras and Wyclef, were always in this music thing for success. She, however, was in it for the love of just writing a song. She said, "I never rewrite, I just write what comes out and that's what this music, hip-hop, means to me: my expression."

That's the way I feel. I don't have any expectations for anyone to live up to.

When we made the *Tougher than Leather* album that coincided with the movie, Run once told me that he couldn't understand why I was so def. After all, he said, "Your rhymes are so simple."

That hurt my feelings, but I didn't let on or confront him. Yet when the album was complete, I went back and listened to the album and because of that conversation, I felt something was missing from my delivery. I was sort of depressed about it.

So I went to Jay to discuss it. "Yo, how are my rhymes on this album? Because it is really starting to mess with me."

Jay had the answer. "Are you stupid? Eric B. and Rakim were flipping over everything you said."

Then I started to realize. What made me def wasn't that I was the best vocalist or anything, or that I got more rhymes than LL Cool J, or that I was dominant and loud like Chuck D. It was that I was always sincere about what I said.

Like Jay told me, "D, everybody loves you, because your fans, they can say all your rhymes."

Battling the emotional responses that come with constantly being judged are something all of us go through. Maybe, to a degree, entertainers go through it a bit more because the whole world is judging our work in very public forums: radio, TV, magazines, newspapers.

I used to deal with things by bottling them up. Then I'd medicate myself with drugs or alcohol to ease the pain.

When I stopped drinking and using drugs, I still had a need to find solace from somewhere. So, for a time, I turned back to an old childhood friend, religion.

I am more spiritual than into organized religion, but I have read the Bible nine times. I read it nine times to really get what Jesus said. I didn't want to take anyone's word for it.

I went to Catholic school all my life. Catholic elementary, Catholic high school, and a Catholic college. Learningwise, it was a good time. There was too much in public schools that could have disrupted my attention.

Neither of my parents were Catholic, but they realized that the discipline of the private school was what I needed. But as far as *being* a Catholic, it was always more like a course to me than what I was. I grew up Catholic because that was what I was put into. So I obeyed the rules to it.

I went through Communion and the rituals, but that's because I was put into it. I never really thought about it.

All my life I had math, history, geometry, and religion. That's how it was. It wasn't like my culture. It was another course I just wanted to pass. I thought of that even up to my college years.

It was purely academic. It was never holy and sacred and something that contained the answers.

There was a time when Run-DMC was publicly being known as "born again" into the Christian faith.

Run was the first to get so-called born again. He joined a nondenominational church, Zoe Ministries, 103rd and Riverside Drive in Manhattan, and was going there for almost two years before I got there. He never forced it on me and never came off as a religious fanatic or any of that stuff.

He was just persistent. "You need to come, you need to come." Run was really into the program, but I suspected that it wasn't so much spirituality that was moving him as it was the orderly nature of the church. You follow the rules, good things will happen to you. And Run, who had been through a lot of things in the last few years before he joined the church, followed the program to the letter.

The first day I went there, the minister said, "Whoever wants to give their life to God, come up to the front."

So I went. I mean, to me, it was nothing outstanding about declaring that you loved God. I thought, all right. I'll go up there and say the words, because I felt that it was something that's part of everyday churchgoing.

Maybe I didn't understand the implications. But all of a sudden, I had made a bigger commitment than I had anticipated, or desired.

At first, I enjoyed going to the church, because it was unlike any religious situations I had been through.

The bishop of the church was a great man. I loved sitting there because it was almost like being back in college. He was teaching me about life. So I went there often for a time, to the point where people were asking me if I would also become a minister after Run declared himself a reverend.

But unlike Run, I had qualms. How does anyone else know what is good for me? In my heart, I knew I was not a minister. I was not doing what Run was doing, believing in the church to the point where it became my life. But everyone wanted to see that happen because Run was doing it. It made a nice story.

And that's when it started getting shaky to me, my entire relationship to life and particularly to Run-DMC. It was almost like God was telling me, "All right. Your work here is done."

After a while, I realized that this church was no longer the place for me. It served me well and taught me some good things. And as I gradually woke up to that, I started reading a lot of books on spirituality and metaphysics, books that would analyze what Jesus said in the Bible.

I came to the conclusion that whoever Jesus was, he didn't think the measure of a good person was their church attendance record. In fact, he was saying the opposite. God is not in the temple. The words and utterances made in church are empty unless it's in your heart, and everything that is written in the Bible is already written in your heart. The printed page is only written for the people that need instruction.

The more I got into it, the less I liked organized religion. Titles, rituals, and levels of administrators, it's all wrong. If you believe in that sort of hierarchical approach, then you'll have to condemn the person that goes to another church or believes something different.

But the first thing Christ told us was to not judge someone else. So how are you going to say what they're doing is wrong?

When I've traveled elsewhere around the world, I've been exposed to other faiths and beliefs. I've studied some Buddhism. What I've found is all truths are parallel. Each religion has a message of tolerance, of nonviolence, of charity toward those that need your help.

So I've adopted a philosophy that all that you need to know about the universe or God or whatever you want to call it is within you. That's why I don't like everybody getting together and worshiping the same way. I don't think that's what God is, nor are buildings, books, or entrenched codes of conduct.

In a way, I knew what Jesse Ventura was saying when he claimed religion was for weak-minded people. But I wouldn't say "weak." It's just for people who need a little guidance in life. But to me, organized religion is like another political organization. A lot of people feel that they're doing all they can do to show their faith by showing up for one hour a week at some location, church. Me, I'd much rather take a bit of knowledge and use it in the world and see if it will work.

I guess my experience at Zoe Ministries really started to go sour when they started calling me to find out why I was not coming to church. I am not coming because I am not coming! I have to come there to find God? I don't like that. I can find God by sitting here in this room and just thinking. Even Moses said that all that you would know about God is within you.

The experience with the church has made me very cynical

about the whole process. I think that anything that somebody organizes because they had an idea, whether it's about God or not, I think it's all somebody just trying to cash in. It's a power thing.

I am just going to live by example. Even Jesus said to live your life by example. That's the greatest gospel.

That's why you should be skeptical the next time you see a televised awards show and the winners are thanking God.

A lot of them are saying it because it's become reflexive. It's like, all right, let me thank God, because that's the thing to do. I've done it myself—got to remember to thank God.

I haven't known too many truly religious people in show business. Not to judge anybody, but everybody claims they are religious because they sang in the church when they were younger. But now they're running wild with all sorts of behavior that most people wouldn't call religious.

One of the main points I've taken from the books I've read, including the Koran and the Bible, is that the elaborate, public display of faith is usually the phoniest behavior.

Like Jesus says, "So what that you wear the long robe?" So what that you know all the Scriptures, that you say your prayers aloud? God doesn't care about that. The prayer that you say in your closet that nobody else knows about is the most sincere. Only God knows.

As for my son, I'm really trying hard to not let him get mixed up in classifications. I know there's going to be a day when he comes to me and says, "Daddy, what am I?"

I'm just going to say, "You're a child of God, son."

I think he's already getting that, at least subliminally. Right now, my son attends a Christian private school, where they teach him the basics of the faith, but don't dig too deeply into it. I'm hoping that he becomes curious enough to explore on his own. I want him to have a universal understanding of religion.

And he's shown signs of insight.

The other day, he told me that when the daddy is too mean to the son, that's a sin against God.

I said, "No, it's not."

He said, "It is to me."

And as I thought about it, I agreed. It is to him. And God gave him the right to decide.

That's the greatest gospel of them all.

While the organized part of religion didn't prove to be the solution for me, I did find great strength in spirituality. I'm a voracious reader, and I devour all sorts of books on spirituality and metaphysics while we're on tour.

As a result, as I grow older I've discovered a better way to deal with the problems and pressures of everyday life. Once a week, I try to take the time to count my blessings. It's a simple solution, but one that works for me. And I believe it can work for all of us, no matter how humble our lives or circumstances may be.

I make a conscious effort to make myself feel good. I'll sit back and reflect on everything that I don't like or is making me upset at that moment. Everything. Which can sometimes be a lot, depending on what's going on at the moment. I'm sure you know the feeling.

After I review everything that I wish wasn't there in my life, things I wish I could change, everything that I believe is wrong, things that I don't agree with that are going on in my life—after thinking about all that stuff, I tell myself that it's nothing compared to this beautiful sunshine. Or this nice rainy day. Maybe I tell myself I'm going to the store right now to just do some shopping. Or read to my son.

The key is, I can put what I believe is all the bad stuff in my life in a bag, push it aside, and let it go.

Sometimes that's tougher than others. At one point in the last year, it was really tough. Because I was deciding about Run-DMC.

It was during a period where it seemed like everything in my life was pointing out the turmoil that comes with being in a major group. I spent my time reading books on the Beatles, watching those shows on VH1 that detail what goes on "Behind the Music," sitting back and reflecting on the times we had as Run-DMC.

The conclusion I came to was that I am at a point where I don't want to be in Run-DMC anymore, at least as a recording unit. I can do the tours because that's fun and I know those songs. That's something that I can do forever.

But I am at a point now where I'm saying I am wrong if I don't really make a decision on it. If I'm just doing it to get the group work, then it's wrong.

It took me a while to be able to come to this point. In the past I was always the guy who just let things run and didn't complain. That builds up over time. It led me to seek help from a professional about two years ago.

When I went to see the psychiatrist, she was asking me things like, "Oh, so you think it's selfish to do what's good for you? You think it's wrong for a person to do what's good for them?"

I said, "Yeah," because you are supposed to be a team player. But she helped me to see that everyone that surrounded me— my record company, my partners, my prior management—everybody around me was doing it for themselves. And she made me understand: since everybody around me is doing something for themselves and no one is caring about me, that's why I was sitting there talking to her.

I had so much respect for everyone around me, I started losing respect for myself.

I think a lot of people do that. That's why a lot of people end up messed up in life.

A lot of the problems in life are caused by a lack of respect for self. Once you respect yourself, then you will respect the other person in the way that you wish to be respected. It's a delicate balancing act, and one the world may never master. But until you do that, everything is going to go haywire.

You see it all the time in professional sports and entertainment. Take the Orlando Magic basketball team of a few years ago. They made the NBA finals with such young stars as Shaquille O'Neal, Penny Hardaway, and Dennis Scott. This was a powerhouse team, one that could have been a winner for years.

But playing as a team requires some people to defer to others. Shaquille and Penny clashed because both wanted to dominate the team and the ball.

We all know how it turned out. Shaq went to live in L.A., where he had a world of opportunities. Penny deteriorated, injured himself, and wound up heading to Phoenix.

Today, the Magic are a struggling NBA team.

Now, many people I talk to say that both of them are wrong. But they had to make a decision in their search for self-respect. It was a tough decision, but it was one that they had to make in order to be true to themselves.

It's funny that I became the person who deferred and repressed his feelings. Because I've always been accused of being physically intimidating.

I've never been in a physical fight. Nobody ever really pushed me over the line, although I came close several times.

Unless I'm defending my well-being or family, physical confrontation would only take away from where I am going. That means that this person has something I think I can't get.

When you fight for your respect, you are actually saying to yourself and to the universe that something is unattainable for you.

One of the interesting things about being a performer is the notion that you're a success or a failure based on the amount of records you're selling at the moment.

My definition of failure is not being unable to accomplish everything that you set out to do. I believe failure is not finding the truth that lies in every experience.

Somebody who runs a marathon but comes in ninety-ninth

isn't a failure. Even though the person who won got the trophy and the money and the endorsements, the person who came in ninety-ninth won because he has accomplished something just by finishing the race. He wasn't defeated. Rather, he didn't achieve everything that was possible. But it's highly likely that, using the knowledge and experience that he gained from the situation, he will come back stronger and better next time. I think failure is education. You find out what something is like and learn from it.

It amazes me sometimes what people regard as a failure.

I don't think anyone is a failure. I mean, take a kid in the fourth grade who just can't read. He's labeled as stupid by some people, and largely given up on, even at that early age.

But there are many paths to the same goal. He just has to take another path to get to the same place another kid is heading. If anything is a failure, it's that we as a society have too many rules, regulations, and laws and not enough encouragement.

Nobody fails, because what you are saying when you label someone a failure is that there is only one way, and I don't agree with that.

I've never felt that I was a failure in life, even when I didn't achieve everything that I have hoped and dreamed would happen. And while that's a good attitude to have, I also want to point out that I'm not advocating that you ignore reality and pat people on the back when they give little or no effort. I'm not a big fan of telling people lies in order to make them feel better.

I'm just advocating encouragement over discouragement. And that strategy can assume many forms.

When I was in the eleventh grade, I did very well in math. Algebra was harder, and geometry and all the more advanced mathematics were even harder. But I did all right.

Then I reached trigonometry and I got an F! An F! This was unheard-of for me. I was largely an A student in my classes.

One of the teachers in my all-boys Catholic school was very mean about it. He ran his class like a boot camp, and I guess he didn't want any of the recruits to let him down by doing poorly.

He was a chemistry teacher, and I had failed trigonometry and wasn't doing particularly well in chemistry. He seemed to take it personally that I had done so poorly.

So he pulled me into his office and went off on me. He's like, "You are stupid, you're dumb, get out of my face." I mean, he was screaming!

I have no idea why he was so worked up about this.

Worse, he didn't offer any solutions or any particular insights. He certainly didn't offer any help to me. But I think he knew what button he was pushing.

I got mad at him for labeling me a lost cause and said to myself that I was at least going to pass his class, if only to show him that he wasn't right about me.

I think at first I got a C in chemistry and then I went up to a B, and finally I got an A minus.

I was like, yeah, all right. But that still didn't solve my trigo-nometry problem.

Another Irish Christian brother at the school was a little older than my chemistry teacher. He was maybe in his fifties, where the other guy who screamed at me was around twenty-eight years old.

He tried a different tactic. He pulled me aside in the hallway and talked to me very nicely. "Darryl, I know you can pass. From looking at your records and your progress in this school, I know you can do it. Your parents are paying all this money for you to go to private school, so why don't you try just a bit harder and see what happens." With that, he put on his glasses and walked away.

From there, I rededicated myself to my studies, and wound up getting an A plus in trigonometry.

In both cases, the lectures brought out the talent that I had within myself and made me apply it. And while both of them tried to point out that I was failing, they also wanted to wake me up to the fact that I was *not* a *failure*. I was merely not applying myself in the way that I needed to apply myself to achieve my fullest potential.

Hey, everyone has peaks and valleys in their achievements. A baseball pitcher can have a bad game. An author can follow a best-seller with something that sells a lot less.

And believe me, a recording artist can be on the top of the charts and off the charts within a few years.

But I have to laugh when I see someone say things about an artist like Alanis Morissette. She sold ten million records on her first album, three million on her second, and some people said, "What a failure!" What are people thinking?

When Run-DMC went from selling three million units with *Raising Hell* to one and a half million with *Tougher than Leather*, a lot of people—okay, practically everybody—was saying Run-DMC is over.

Run got all depressed and was suicidal. His brother, Russell, screamed at him after he actually attempted to do away with himself.

"Do you know how many people would want to sell a million and a half records?" Russell raged. "Do you know what you're throwing away?"

What Run didn't realize is that how many albums he sold at any particular moment couldn't take away from what he had already achieved. We were already Run-DMC, and when people talked about us, it wouldn't be about our failures, but our successes.

Hey, Run-DMC can do this for the rest of our lives. The money may change, or the places we play, and the circumstances of our recording contract may differ.

But we can be happy. I might be happy selling three hundred thousand records. I am not going to let anybody tell me I failed. It takes me to say I failed.

The Root of All Evil

Let's talk about a dirty topic: money. It's the way that most of the world keeps score.

A lot of people in this world are obviously obsessed by money, by how much they now have, how much they once had, and how much they will someday earn.

To me, money always represented what I could get with it. Not any particular power or status. Merely that it was the thing that I had to exchange for obtaining whatever it was that I wanted. That's all it meant.

I admit, I'm not really good with money. My first million dollars was actually a tribute to my mother and father caring enough about me to not let me spend too much of it. They made me put some money away when it was rolling in, and for that I am grateful. As working-class people, they knew the value of a dollar.

I'm glad they did. Because I never really cared about it. Even now, as an adult, a husband and father with a mortgage and bills to pay, it's not an obsession.

I look at my son and think I have to get money to make sure he's provided for. But that's the extent of it, because I don't really care all that much. I've always felt that my wealth is my creativity. However much money I have or don't have at the moment isn't a reflection of anything other than the circumstances of the moment.

I had like three bank accounts when Run-DMC was in its earning prime. Once my parents knew how much I was making, and saw how foolishly I was spending it, they made sure two of the accounts were inaccessible, which was all right by me. There was enough in the one account that I had.

I was pretty immature back then about my earnings. I remember I used to take my friends to the bank and then show them the statement. "Look. This motherfucker got sixty-five thousand dollars in it!" And they'd look at it like, that's more money than any two of them were making. You know what I'm saying?

I didn't lord it over them. I was always generous. I'd take everybody out and shop for them and buy food and plane tickets and this and that.

My mom always said I was too generous. When I was young, she'd give me seven dollars for my allowance. I would go spend six on my friends. Constantly. She was so amused by that.

As I started getting older, she wasn't so amused at my spending habits, particularly when I became DMC and began getting some real money. She would always encourage me to save and not waste. That was the constant refrain: you spend too much money, you spend too much money. It's a mother's way, I guess.

When we were about to sign our new record deal with Arista, my mom tried a different tactic. We're sitting around the dinner table and she wasn't talking to me about the money.

The Root of All Evil

She started talking to my wife. It took me back to when I was seven years old.

Sometimes I think I over-tip. If the cab ride is $9.50, I might give the guy $20.00. But I'm really not that extravagant in my personal life. At least not anymore.

When I was younger and first came into money, I bought a Cadillac and a big monster truck with a fifty-thousand-dollar sound system. My father told me it was the most ridiculous thing I ever did.

Now I look back on it and have to agree with him, because I paid fifty thousand dollars for the sound system and it never worked! I drove the truck away from the car stereo place, and the next week I was back there for repairs, the beginning of an endless cycle of purported fixes and returns for more repairs. It never worked.

It was more than a little embarrassing. I remember hanging with Parrish from EPMD. He said he wasn't putting a system in his car, since he had paid two thousand dollars for one that never worked. "I'm just sticking with the factory unit," he said. "It don't need to be loud anyway."

I'm standing there thinking to myself, "You jerk. You paid fifty thousand dollars and it never worked."

I guess it wasn't meant to be. To top it off, when it finally stopped working and I didn't care about fixing it again, someone broke into the truck and took it.

My wife and me discuss finances a lot. But we don't argue over money, like a lot of couples do. I just let her control it.

I realize the importance of money, but to me, it's still not the most important thing in my life. I understand that my son and wife need it, and I'm just thankful that I'm able to earn it.

But I've seen too many people obsess about money to the point where it rules their lives.

Russell Simmons sold his interest in Def Jam Records for a reported one hundred million. Yet Run always says Russell is cheap. My hunch is he's just being smart, and doesn't want to keep giving Run money. Run's attitude is, "I'm your brother! I'm supposed to be rich too!"

But Russell is a guy who always wants more money. He says that in all his interviews. But that's the problem—once people get a lot of money, they want more.

I do not covet money. I don't wake up saying, "I want more money," or even, "I want money." The times I did start thinking like that, I started losing it, because I kept telling myself I need more and more and I was stressing myself out trying to get it.

Although I wish I had made some better investments with my money from the period of Run-DMC's greatest success, there are also reasons I'm kind of glad that I didn't. For instance, sometimes I wish I'd bought a house, but then I realize what a hard time I would have had getting rid of all the people in the house once my life changed.

If all my money left tomorrow, I wouldn't miss it. In fact, at least technically, in the eyes of the law it all did disappear at one point.

Yes, there was a bankruptcy.

That came in mid-1990, a time when all of us in the group were in financial trouble.

When we did the *Back from Hell* album, things were looking grim. We were in another one of our seemingly perpetual fights with Profile Records, the album had flopped, Run was going to church a lot but still struggling with some problems, and things were generally drying up.

Because of the dispute with Profile, we decided that we weren't going to make any more Run-DMC albums. That was our only leverage—withhold our services.

We talked about doing solo careers. Run had gained a lot of weight, so he was going to go out as Fat Joe. Me? Well, when Russell and everyone asked me what I was going to do, I said I'll make a record. Jay will produce it. Or whatever.

Tell you the truth, I never got around to it.

But we were becoming obsessed with our contract situation.

Honestly, I don't know why it came to the point that it did. It was like, "Okay. You ain't gonna change the contract? Then if we don't ever make a record, we just never make a record." They could hold our contract for life without getting another album.

Without any royalties coming in, and no tours coming up, I had to start living off savings. That led to problems.

Run was the first to declare bankruptcy, but the record company accused him of filing for it as a way to get out of his record contract. You've seen what TLC and a few other groups have gone through. If you go bankrupt, they can't hold you to the deal. That probably delayed things even more than they were already delayed.

And meanwhile, I'm just sitting at home while everything is going to hell. Back from hell and right back to hell.

Finally I had reached the end of my financial rope, and I had to declare bankruptcy as well. They fought me along with Run. And in the end, nobody won. We finally worked it all out and did a new deal.

And then we went into the studio to make *Down with the King*. It was a big comeback album for us; it reasserted our prominence in the rap world and was a platinum record.

After I filed for bankruptcy, my parents helped me get back on my feet. This time, I'm listening a lot more closely to their advice on saving. Maybe not as closely as my mom would like. But I'm listening.

Once we started working on the *Down with the King* record, our problems didn't end. We started beefing again with our record company, who promptly started withholding money again. And we were on the road this time, with expenses piling up. It was a never-ending cycle.

It was illin'.

It was crazy.

It was the record business. Eventually, we got it straightened out. But I don't feel I'll ever be able to really relax in this business. There's too many things that can go wrong.

I still feel bad about the bankruptcy. It makes you feel like a failure, that you should have been wiser in your dealings. I never wanted it to happen, and it would have seemed ridiculous to me that I'd ever have had to do it in the years when we were walking around with fifteen thousand dollars in our pockets.

In the end, I have no one but myself to blame for not paying closer attention to what was happening in my career, not knowing what's out there, what my options were, how closely I was tied in with the other members of the group. I also made the mistake of waiting for Run to straighten out his affairs, rather than going out and making some moves on my own. That would have been wiser than taking every dime that I had earned and having to use it to live. All the money my mother and father made me save up was gone, and it was a pretty nice amount.

But I've learned a great lesson, and I'll share it with you. If you're a performer, or a businessperson, or in a partnership, make sure your assets are in your own corporation and that you have your own manager and accountant. Take care of you, rather than assuming that the group is all in it together. That's just how it's gotta be.

Even if it's your brother. Even if it's your mother. 'Cause when something goes bad, you'll realize that it all comes down to you, anyway.

I often wonder what I would say if I could go back now and talk to me at that age as the person I am now.

Likely, it would be "Make some investments." Also, "Can't you stop drinking and smoking reefer?" That's my first instinct.

But then again, I don't think I would have learned what I learned if I went back and told myself that. I think the more important thing is what happens after you come through that sort of thing. Eventually, either you die or you go to rehab when you're on that schedule.

The Root of All Evil

Money, in the end, is security. I realized that after reading an article on the actor John Travolta. They had asked him that question, "How does it feel to be rich?" He basically said it feels good, but not in the sense that it makes a poor person feel bad. He was like, "It was security for my family."

I'm like, "Yeah, but security gets you your own plane?"

I mean, how much money is enough money? Microsoft leader Bill Gates has more money than anybody on the planet. Does that mean he's the happiest man on earth?

I didn't really examine it back then, but now when I think back, money came to me when I didn't care about it.

I got money for doing something that I truly, truly loved, that I would have been doing, cherishing, holding dear to my heart if I never got the money. And that's the way it should be.

Unfortunately, money isn't that way for a lot of people.

I'm constantly amazed by that, even at this stage of my life. Money is the ultimate motivator to a lot of people, to the point where they don't seem to hear anything else you say.

I remember the time me and my manager and my lawyer went in to see Mr. Clive Davis, the head of my record label, Arista Records, shortly after we signed with them.

He's a record industry legend, the former head of CBS Records and then founder of Arista. He's been credited for masterminding the careers of Whitney Houston, Aretha Franklin, Taylor Dayne, Barry Manilow, and countless other stars.

In short, he's a real record man, a guy who's truly into the music, a man who delights in playing new albums over and over and over for his staff.

I thought I could have a conversation with him about my career and my relationship with Run-DMC at that point in my life. Let me take you with me inside that office.

I went in there and I told him my whole story. I told him everything that I was going through with my fellow partners, how

I love them but I am a frustrated artist. I didn't want to go talk to anyone else about this except him because as I saw it, I was the player going to the coach. I felt that he was the only one who didn't really know me and that this is going to be a chance for him to hear from a previously unknown member of the group.

He looked at me and said, "I hear what you're saying. But your timing could have been a little better. I just spent a million dollars related to your record."

He told me what I didn't want to hear. You are a member, you are a shareholder in a third of this corporation. Right now is not a good time for you to be saying this. You have a chance to make money.

This after I told him that I would shoot myself in the head before I put money as the deciding factor in what is going to make me happy. So he sees that he's not connecting with me, so he goes through this story about Carlos Santana and Santana's new album. It was, of course, one of the big success stories of recent times in the record industry, the comeback album for one of the great guitarists. All engineered by Mr. Davis, who paired Santana with a number of younger artists.

"I spent a million on him, I brought all these other artists in, blah, blah, blah," said Clive. "His album is number one on the charts!"

That's not important to me! I know I can be happy without money because of the fact that I love life and do something that I like. I already proved that that formula works, I told him.

The only reason I am here in your office is because I was writing rhymes in high school and somebody else gave me a record deal. I went along because I liked what I was doing. I didn't do it because it was a record deal, I didn't go because somebody told me he had a check.

But it never registered with Clive. He was listening to a different tune. Clive Davis is no longer at Arista. He has a new label and L. A. Reid of Laface is now the new head of Arista.

The Root of All Evil

When I hear a song like Puff Daddy's "It's All about the Benjamins," it bothers me.

The reason the song bothers me is that it gives the impression that that's all life is about. You're telling these kids that are sitting there watching you with your diamonds, your Benz, your clothes, and your lifestyle that all you have to care about in life is money.

In other words, you have to do whatever it takes, by any means necessary, to get to be like Puffy. And if you don't have the talent of someone like Puffy, then what you can do is go out and sell drugs, because, after all, it's all about money.

Well, guess what? Life is not all about the Benjamins. It's okay to want some Benjamins, but what about education? What about respecting people? What about a nice walk through the woods? What about having fun, a picnic, or anything else that can be had for nothing?

I saw a poster that's out recently, and I think its message is fantastic. It says it doesn't matter how much money I made or how many things I have accumulated in life. All that matters in the end is the impact I had on the life of a child.

When you say it's all about the Benjamins, especially to a rap-buying audience that's primarily filled with millions of young people, you're telling a whole bunch of poor cats who want to be where you are that money will get you there.

I respect Puffy for what he accomplished as a businessman. But I don't agree with putting a record out there like that, without backing it up with recordings that provide understanding.

I know it sounds trite. But please don't worry about money.

I know you can only say that if you have it, and if you haven't got it then you're going to worry. Because even rich people worry about money.

And that's the problem. Once people get a lot of money, they want more, instead of just asking how they can move this money around to help benefit others.

Because if you can make that money once, you can make it

again. Some people get money and the thought that their money is going to leave them is so devastating, they can't bear to part with it.

I've heard a theory that if all the money on the planet was divided equally among every human being, that in five years the same people who were wealthy before the money was distributed would regain all their wealth.

The theory is that the people who make a lot of money focus on that and are good at it. Frankly, I think it's more likely that those are the people who are obsessed with it, and who will do anything to have it.

I've had money, not had money, had money again. And what I've come to realize is that money is just a symbol. In fact, at a certain point in life, when you're finally an adult, you might even say it's a magnifier. When an adult gets a lot of money, you can see what he really is by how he acts with it.

The key is to be the same, vibrant person no matter how much money you have. If you can do that, you'll always be wealthy.

I watch people in the entertainment business and realize money is killing them.

They're trying so hard to get it and they're so worried about losing it that they never really enjoy themselves. I say these people are destroying themselves because what they are saying is "I want more, I want, I don't have, I got to get. . . ." Essentially, what they're saying is their whole existence isn't right. They can't enjoy the moment because it's all about what will happen in the future. And they're never going to be secure, so when will they find peace? The truth is no amount of money will fill up that hole inside them. No amount will ever bring stability.

Because it isn't about a specific amount of money.

It's about them.

Money is an amplifier. If you were a jerk before you got money, you'll be a jerk with money, only more so because you'll undoubtedly use that newfound wealth to promote the qualities that made you a jerk in the first place. It brings out your true colors.

I've pretty much always lived the same, no matter how much money I had. We might have had more luxury items, more drugs, more of this and that, but we were still partying like we always did and surrounded by the same people we always were surrounded by. It wasn't like we developed an interest in yachting or started hanging around different people or moved to Aspen.

I learned a vital lesson about how to behave when money comes into your life after I read an article about the rock singer Meat Loaf. You remember his story—he was on top of the world when *Bat Out of Hell* sold ten million copies and sold out arenas. He was *the* star for about two years.

But then his next album didn't do so well, the touring started to go to smaller and smaller places, and his cash flow started dropping. He parted ways with Jim Steinman, the songwriter for *Bat Out of Hell,* and eventually developed a condition where he couldn't sing.

Meat Loaf was feeling tremendously depressed. It had all gone away in a flash for him, and he felt that he was no longer important because he wasn't earning millions of dollars as a rock star.

But when he went out in public, the people he met weren't seeing Meat Loaf, the failure.

No, they would see the man they remembered as having sold ten million records and put on one of the best shows in rock 'n' roll. They saw someone they considered a star, no matter what his current circumstances were.

Meat Loaf had a hard time grasping it when people told him he was acting funny. He didn't realize that he was acting different. He thought the fans had abandoned him, when, in fact, he had created a situation where they couldn't show him how much they loved him. It's not surprising that, after he recovered his voice and reunited with Jim Steinman, he had one of the comeback albums of the year.

The point is that money and fame doesn't make a person a

star. Only they can convince themselves of that. That's why the poorest person can walk in a room and have star quality, while someone with a lot of jewelry and furs can come off as tacky.

Having to rely on money or the things money can buy is a confidence problem. People think the money is making them legit, but it's really that they don't have a sense of wealth inside them, so they surround themselves with these things that other people consider wealthy, in order to impress.

But it leaves their own soul poor.

I think the true goal of money should be to use it to leave a foundation for someone to build on. That way, money isn't all about listing what you own.

I think it is important that you take money and use it to further causes. Perhaps open schools, hospitals, give people jobs, generally enhance society. Not just for yourself and your family. I'm talking about everybody.

Most of the people with money just die and leave it to their child and then that child dies and leaves it to the next child, and in the midst of all that the whole family is fighting for it.

But if they start moving it around, it will generate enough for everybody.

One of the sad things about the way the record industry has become is that making music for a lot of people has become a day job. I hear kids say all the time that they want to make records so they can get paid.

No, you want to make records to express yourself and teach people and let people know what you think, to create and leave something in the world.

I know what I'm speaking about. Because I believe the love of money changed the Run-DMC situation.

Time for a Change

One of the lessons that all religions teach is forgiveness.

And in the last year, I've had to apply that lesson constantly to my own situation.

Forgiveness is a big thing. It's one of the greatest gifts you can give someone.

I have read a lot of books about forgiveness. Forgiveness is immediate. You have to be able to forgive a person right then and there. You can't forgive a person if it takes months and years to reach that point. If you cannot forgive a person right then and there, the same day it happened, the dominant feeling isn't sincere. It's grudging. And you've harbored all those feelings for so long, eating away at you.

Let's take one small example. If I hadn't been able to forgive Run then and there when he was giving me grief about the Beastie Boys, or forgive the Beastie Boys for real or imagined slights, my life could have been so much different.

There is so much we could never have accomplished, experiences we never would have had. We never would have continued past that point. And that's just one tiny fraction of my career. Imagine the consequences, say, if Run hadn't forgiven *me* for getting so drunk at our first gig. So you get my point.

Forgiveness plays a role in respecting a person for what he is. My attitude has always been, "Cool. That's the way you feel? I still love you." I'm still able to stand next to that person.

My philosophy was put to a severe test when it came to Run-DMC's projects over the last few years.

Our label, Profile Records, had been drifting for some time. They were looking to be bought out by a larger label. But in order to get the price that they wanted, they had to have a viable Run-DMC album at least ready to roll, to show that the label's all-time number one act was still ready to get in the game. That would have added appreciably to the label's value.

At the time, though, I was experiencing some troubles with my vocal cords. I never really had much vocal training, and as a result, I developed a condition common to a lot of people who sing or talk extensively for a living. I strained my vocal cords.

We tried to do some things in the studio, but my voice just wasn't the same. Thus, we couldn't really deliver anything to Profile, and the label was getting really worried that their prospects for a sale were drying up.

So they came to Run with a proposition: start work on an album, and we'll pay you a certain amount of money as you deliver us completed tracks. We'll tell people you're working on a Run-DMC album.

Run needed the money. I did too, so I understand.

But he made a bad decision. Instead of coming to me and

explaining the situation, or telling me he was doing a record without me until my voice gets better, he just went ahead and did it.

I actually found out that this was happening because another person at Profile told me, thinking I already knew. And in the meantime, I had been reluctant to do anything but work on getting better, because I felt I had a commitment to him and the group, and I was going to fulfill it.

Someone asked me what would make him play me like that. Why would someone do that after all we'd been through, all we'd accomplished as the guys who made rap? Why wouldn't he come and say, "Yo, I'm going to make an album with Profile"?

I'll tell you why. Because he thought I'd be jealous they were giving him money.

It would have helped me a lot if he would have told me that was what he was doing. Then I could have been out there trying to book things for myself; lectures or other projects. That would have given me permission to go be who I need to be and not worry about my guys.

But they went ahead and didn't even consult me. Profile was sold to Arista Records for many millions of dollars, based on the expectation of a Run-DMC record.

I recovered my vocals, but I struggled with the concept of returning to the studio. How could I after what I'd been through? Was I supposed to say, "Oh, Profile is going to Arista, and they promised all this money"? Now I just return to the team and go on and make an album and act like things are all right?

Once that went down, things were all right when we were touring because that's a situation where each member is putting something in to make this thing work.

But the recording process is different. It requires cooperation in a way that is difficult if there isn't trust. And while I'm not mad and I understand why they did it, there's just nothing there for me anymore.

All good things come to an end. And I've been sitting around for the last three years saying I don't want to do Run-DMC anymore. My eyes have been opened by the incident with the album, but it's about more than that.

Run didn't understand. He thought I was trying to screw up his career. He told me, "You are messing my money up."

I'm sorry he feels that way. But it goes deeper than that. If you've ever wondered how successful groups break up, I'll shed a little light on it for you. It's never about the money, although that can be one of the symptoms. No, it's always about growth, or the lack of it.

When I look at Run these days, we only connect when we're together during a live stage performance. Because that's something that we did together for so many years that it's unchangeable, unbreakable. But there comes a point where it's time to move on in other aspects of your life.

I can't do anything anymore with the love that I had when it was being built.

I am now thirty-five years old. I want the respect that's due me as a thirty-year-old, not the respect I once achieved as a young rapper and hip-hop guy. Don't want that from my fans or the person I meet on the street.

I am at a point now where I have to start doing what thirty-five-year-old musicians should be doing. I don't have the same fans as Canibus or any of the young hip-hoppers.

Aging isn't something to be feared. If you're afraid to age, you're going to have problems. Mentally, emotionally, physically. But if you're not scared of the unknown, you will never age.

When I came out of the hospital after my bout with pancreatitis, I felt reborn. I was drug-free, cleaned up; my mind and everything was clear. I started exercising and being careful with my diet. As a result, I look younger than I did before I went into the hospital. I mean, if you look at me in 1983 and look at me now, I look the same. But in those years in between, I looked very old.

Aging or feeling old, like poverty, is a state of mind. Aging is actually wonderful. You know why? Because there is the mystery of the unknown. What will I do next? And the eagerness and the excitement of discovering new things will refresh your soul. The reason why you're so vibrant when you're young is that everything that happens is so interesting to you. So why not keep it that way when you get old? You don't know what's going to happen until tomorrow.

I think my groupmates are afraid of what they would do if they didn't have Run-DMC. I felt out of place during the making of our latest album, because the direction certain people wanted us to take was get with the new guys and you'll sell records.

So you see how people just do stuff for money. Frankly, I don't agree with that. Why should I? If I was to tell Run, who's a minister, "All right, yo! Just come on down 'cause I got this thing I'm doing with the devil! I'm doing a deal with the devil."

No! He's not going to come. He's not. And he wouldn't do that for the money.

That's not going to work for me. But Run takes it as a challenge. Run's confident enough to go word for word with any of the young MCs because that's what he wants. He wants to impress that crowd. I don't care about that.

I'm saying, dag, Run, Jay, and me could perform forever. And I would love that. When people interview me, I say we want to be doing this forever, till we're eighty.

But making new records and trying to be together? I don't think we can do it anymore. You know, Run is a minister and he's doing his other things and he's got five kids. I only have one. He lives in Queens, I live in Jersey. He likes this; I don't like that no more. And it's like right now is where we need to grow up and experience other things.

Right now I feel like I'm grown. It's time for me to graduate. And I think that happened with the Beatles after being together for eleven wonderful years; it happens with all the bands.

Now we can get together for the rest of our lives and go tour the world. We can tour for three years straight and love each other. But we have to respect each other for what we are now.

The first time I brought it up to Run was at our record distributor's convention at the beginning of 1999. We had just gone over to Arista Records after our old recording home, Profile Records, was sold to them. We were there in San Diego for the BMG convention, which showcased all the new acts that were being distributed through the system, so we had to go out there and perform to whip up enthusiasm about our new album.

This was one of the few times me and Run were alone in a room together. He walked into the room and said, "Yo, this is wild, everything that's happening. This is straight business, VH1's *Behind the Music*." It was kind of prophetic.

When I relayed to him what I was feeling, Run tried to talk me out of it. He was like, "D, I hear that. But just go along for the ride. Let's get our money."

After that first meeting, Run took control. "Let me handle this. I'll get this album made. We'll be all right." The idea was I wouldn't be a troublemaker by announcing my plans, allowing them to use me so they could accomplish what they wanted to accomplish.

I agreed. Then we had a talk over the phone maybe six months later. And it came down to me telling him that everything he was trying to do for this album and everything he was trying to do for our career is not going to work.

He thought I was asking for money.

So now in this situation—which can be any situation, not just music, but in life or a business deal—it becomes a question you have to ask yourself: will you allow yourself to continue to cooperate with these people? Is this going to bring you happiness?

Run and I went back and forth on it, until finally it came down to this. I said, "Let's forget about all that stuff. Let's not talk about it. Let's just talk about people in general and life and what's the right thing to do." And I really broke it down for him, how I was feeling. This talk was person-to-person, me speaking to a guy who I had known since kindergarten and been through so much with.

I asked him, "How would you feel if this was happening to you? And how would you feel if every time you go to somebody looking for the right answer they're telling you, 'Think about the money. Think about the money.' "

It didn't register at first. Russell called and he and Run teamed up on me. They were still concentrating on the material things, with one added difference. They tried to use all of that to say, "Think about your son."

I stood my ground.

"The money's not important, 'cause that don't last. And I don't care if I never get another award." And I was putting it in line with somebody who's working in a regular job. You know, the raise is not that important. The promotion, getting that position is not that important. It will come when the time is right, when I least expect it.

There was so many questions they couldn't answer, and it came down to Run telling me, "D, whatever you want to do, I'll support you. If you want to walk away tomorrow, I'll support you."

I was surprised by that. But I was grateful.

So I made a decision that wasn't a compromise. It wasn't anyone striking a deal. I decided to go along with the group for now, but I'm not going to obligate myself to anything because I might decide to leave tomorrow. I had to let them know that when I wake up right now, the little voice is telling me everything's cool.

The day that voice says, "It's time," I'm outta there.

I could too, even though I'm making some good money with Run-DMC. But all the good money that I make with Run-DMC is on the road. When I'm home, there's nothing there for me. I don't get excited when it's time for me to go to the studio. I don't get excited about us making music together. You know, that was already done.

For the past five years, we only come together and click when it's time for the show. The only thing that we know from one to one hundred me, Joe, and Jay are on the same page when we're onstage. Then we all leave and go our separate ways.

Elvis always said when it stopped being fun, it's time to quit. And when you know you ain't got it, you gotta break up that unit. I don't want Run-DMC to go out in disgrace. We had it and we still got it. And that is something that nobody can touch.

It's almost like the wonderful thing where you can have a marriage for so many years and the two parties can separate and still be good friends, still come to the cookout and still be seen in public laughing and slapping five. I think the group's situation now is giving me a taste of that type of relationship.

So it's time to strike out and set a new course. I'm older, wiser, a far different person than the Darryl McDaniels who came out of Hollis, Queens, and became the King of Rock. And after all we've been through, I can look in the mirror and say I like the guy I'm looking at.

You know what it really means to be a good guy? They always say nice guys finish last. But the nice guy who finishes last still finishes. He's going to be there.

I have this rhyme now, "The last man standing when the smoke is clear / When all the smoke is gone, I'll still be standing here."

When you look at basketball, look at Grant Hill. Everybody hates Grant Hill because of his good image. He'll never be Dennis Rodman, for instance.

But in the end, nice old Grant Hill will still be rich and still have many years in the NBA and still accomplish what everybody else is accomplishing.

Because society likes the forceful and greedy, society has no respect for someone who doesn't pursue that path. Everybody is out there admiring the money-hungry, controlling, rich guys, because that is what this whole capitalist society is based on. If you want to succeed, you've got to be ruthless, and this and that.

The whole music industry was based on conniving, wheeling

and dealing, and stealing. An honest guy could have probably sold all those records too.

And now it's time to test that theory.

So thank you for indulging me these last few pages. I hope you've learned something about what it was like for me during the birth of rap music and my various life issues.

I've arrived at a very special time in my life. I'm about to turn the page, marching forward into the unknown, a little apprehensive but excited at the challenges I face.

I came to my conclusions on what I should do after a lot of careful thought and deliberation. I thought about everything that I've experienced in life, every book that I have read, everything that I have seen happen to the people in the world and on the news. And I believe I arrived at what the most important thing in life is, the secret to your success.

It's you. Yourself!

Yes, you are the most important thing in life. That's the key. And what I mean by that is, whatever you're doing in life, whether it is working in a bank or sweeping the floor, you should do it with love from your heart.

When I look back at everything that I've done, everything that happened around me, everything I was ever successful at, it all happened because I loved doing it.

Like when I was in school. It was easy for me to get an A because I loved just writing in my books. I know that sounds funny, but I couldn't wait to get new books and have new pens and fill those books with words. I loved going to school and it was exciting to me.

When I look at rapping, at why we came out of a basement in Hollis, Queens, to play some of the largest arenas in the world and sell millions of records, it was because success was a by-product of what we loved doing. We didn't set out with those goals in mind. Yes, we were ambitious, but we were doing it for fun. It wasn't to get a record deal, or be able to afford the biggest house.

The same way that I was writing rhymes in my basement and listening to music in my room when I was eleven years old, before I even thought of picking up a mike, is the same way I do it now. And I think that's why I've lasted so long.

Fame came to me while I was doing something that I love. I didn't notice it. That's probably why I made so many mistakes along the way. But that's also why I learned a lot.

The lesson of my life is don't let material things be your goal. Enjoy what you are doing, no matter what it is, because anything you are doing can lead you to where you want to be in life.

Now, I hear what you're saying to yourself. "D, how can sweeping the floor compare to rapping at Madison Square Garden?"

Here's my take: sometimes you find yourself in a position where you know that it is going to be hard to get to a goal overnight.

But if you are happy just being in the moment, and not focused on how miserable you are that you haven't yet achieved what you dream of achieving, you can have peace of mind. The fact that you can make a living is reason enough to have a measure of satisfaction. And if you're fortunate enough to have a roof over your head and something to eat, you're better off than a lot of people. It gives you hope that you can do something better.

Now, you don't have to be satisfied. But as long as you take care of you, everything and anything's a possibility.

So if you are going to sweep the floor, then sweep it with all your heart. Be the best sweeper you can be, because then there's something better around the corner. If you go sweep with an attitude, you're just blocking out any chances of advancement. There is a reward in even the humblest task, or the lowliest beginning.

I know. I was in my basement pretending to be Grandmaster Flash. Never said I wanted to be him, or get a car like him. Just pretending that I could have as much fun.

I liked doing it. I did it to the best of my ability, not trying to impress anyone. And I did it to the point where it made me happy.

Time for a Change

In other words, I swept the floor and it's clean. So tomorrow somebody might come along and say, "Who swept this floor? Come here. How would like to be the supervisor?" Just because of your job well done.

Ask yourself how you can improve yourself. How can you be a better person tomorrow? Let me relate that to some of the people who have influenced my life in the last five years. Let me talk about Will Smith and Lauryn Hill.

The last five years were among the worst five years of my life. The music that once brought me joy had lost a lot of the magic for me. Being in Run-DMC, being in the music industry—it was just wearing me down. It had become a job.

As a result, I started having ill will towards other people. That is, until I realized these other people are not the ones empowered to mess up my life. I am.

It is not important what they think of me or what they can give me. I am the most important person to me right now. And it dawned on me that my friend Will Smith was a prime example of doing something that he wanted to do, rather than doing what others thought he should.

Will Smith, when he came out with "Parents Just Don't Understand," was enormously successful. But it was so different than what everybody else was doing in rap at the time, particularly when gangsta rap came out.

Oh, he heard it. "Will Smith is fake. He's phony. He's commercial. He's not rap. He's not hip-hop." All of that stuff. Forced him to go into hiding a little bit, if you can call being a successful actor hiding.

But during his television career on *The Fresh Prince of Bel-Air,* and while his movie career started to take off, he reached a point where he asked himself about music again. What could he do that would make him successful again in that area?

The answer was simple. Just be that same guy as a rapper as you were when you started out, the guy that the audience loves in *The Fresh Prince* and on the big screen.

That's when he came back into rap. He didn't come back any

different from what he was before. He came back being real and being truthful, as nothing more than Will Smith from Philly.

The message: you don't have to change. You don't have to compromise. You don't have to write music that you don't like.

The same thing with Lauryn Hill. She came out with an honest record. She didn't try to give the market what the market wants. She came out totally from left field, sold all those records, and had her baby when people were telling her not to have her baby.

Both Will and Lauryn did what they wanted to do, not what they thought they had to do to sell more records than the next act, or to be something they were not.

In many ways, they threw away everything that made them Hollywood, and came out really honest. Because they were being true to themselves, they were being true to the whole world, and people could respect that.

I hope, as I embark on this new phase of my career, that I can learn from everything that happened to Will Smith and to Lauryn Hill.

Yes, it is very hard to do. It's easier to be negative than positive. Frankly, people think you're a little crazy when you're positive.

That's why it'll be harder for me—or anyone—to break away from anything that has worked in the past. You become a slave to the idea of "If I don't do it this way, I won't be successful. If I don't do it this way, I won't get a check. If I don't do it this way, I won't sell records. If I don't do it this way, nobody will like me."

That's how my mentality was before I decided to take control.

I had lost the ideas and the personality that I had when I first came into this business. I was too busy trying to re-create something that no longer exists, the eighteen-year-old guy from Hollis, Queens. I didn't think anything else would work.

Well, I'm about to find out what will and what won't work.

Now that I'm thinking about my own career, I've heard things said about myself. "Oh, D's flipping now."

But when I was high, running around not caring about anything or anybody that I should have been caring about, they thought I was cool. Funny, isn't it?

If you want to change your life, take small steps. Because if you take big steps, you're liable to overstep something. I don't want anybody to miss the lessons that they can draw from everyday life.

When you move too fast, you miss a lot. Bob Dylan said it best: "I was so much older then / I'm younger than that now."

Look at all the areas in life that need to be better, and not that need to be better because you'll make me or anybody else happy. Make yourself happy.

Everybody has an area in life that could be better. What's good for me might not be good for you. But live your life how you feel will best allow you to accomplish the things you want to accomplish. Not how I say you should do them, but how you should do them. I am just an example. I think you should deal with the person in the mirror first.

People look at me and others like me because I am on TV and stuff like that. But you have people looking at you no matter what you do.

There are people who can hopefully learn from your existence. Maybe you can answer their questions by example.

Whenever you look to criticize, look inside yourself. Take the spite out of your eye before you try to take it out of somebody else's. Don't look for another man's approval, because when you look for another man's approval, it's another form of judging. And judging is not an absolute measure. Because one man might approve of what you are doing and the next man might not.

In order to make everything else better, you got to straighten yourself out. I think people need to work on their own universe, their own little world that God put them in.

That's for the individual. Our society is another matter.

Our culture is spreading out across the world. We're creating a hip-hop planet, and even in the far reaches of Asia, rap music is now becoming mainstream culture. People want to be like Americans because they see how much we enjoy life.

As a result of that spreading hip-hop culture, other good things are happening. I think society is becoming more racially sensitive. Maybe not on a political level, and certainly not yet on an economic level, but our culture is opening up a lot of hearts and minds.

When you turn on MTV now, you can sense that there's a level of respect for all, regardless of where they're from, their sexual orientation, their skin color.

But despite these developments, not enough of society is growing. It's not yet society as a whole. It's select individuals and groups that are becoming sensitive.

I think my generation is leading the way. That might be why we're seeing a backlash from those under twenty-two, the followers of heavier acts like Korn and Limp Bizkit. No one wants to follow their elders, so they rebel. I hope, as they get older, they'll see the wisdom of building up rather than tearing down.

I would hope we can make progress from within. Within each community, there is a small but growing sensitivity, a rejection of the ruthlessness that seems to have been behind the so-called success stories of a lot of famous people that are held up as examples in our society.

I hope I'm seeing the beginnings of a movement away from the embrace of ruthless behavior, one that is moneycentric, market-driven, and about doing everything but the right thing. Look to the honest guys, the men and women who are true to themselves, who are trying to lead by example because they know that following their own path is the way to happiness.

I say first make it good for you. Then you can make it good for me. And then we can truly make it good for all of us.